ANITA WASHINGTON

FAMILY
—IS NOT—
Everything

HOW TO MINIMIZE THEIR MESS, MAXIMIZE YOUR HAPPINESS AND ENJOY EMOTIONAL BAGGAGE BREAKTHROUGHS

Cover design by www.ebooklaunch.com
Cover image by Natalia Hubbert
Interior formatting by We Got You Covered Book Design

YOU CAN GO FROM EMOTIONALLY DRAINED TO EMOTIONALLY HEALTHY AND HAPPY IN JUST 7 STEPS

HAVE YOU EVER WONDERED WHY YOU CAN ONLY REACH A CERTAIN LEVEL OF SUCCESS? WHAT IF I TOLD YOU IT WAS INSIDE OF YOU? WHAT IF I TOLD YOU THAT YOU COULD BEAT EMOTIONAL BAGGAGE AND ENJOY A MEANINGFUL LIFE?

Leave the pain of the past behind and create a re-vision for your future, accomplishing your goals, reaching new success, adding new meaning to your life, and bringing value to the world. Just imagine all the wonderful things your new life can be!

Anita Washington, M.Ed., M.B.A., owner and CEO of That Anita Live LLC, your personal resource for emotional healing and wellness, has taken her counseling expertise and personal experience with childhood trauma turning into adult dysfunctional behavior and identified a seven-step repeatable method to resolve emotional baggage. It has not only worked for her and her previous clients, it can also work for you.

In this book you will:

> ✔ Be **EQUIPPED** to boldly go beyond your comfort zone and refresh, reinvent, and revise your life for the better.

> ✔ Learn how to **TRANSFORM** negative thinking into positive thinking with 7 affirmations, 7 results-driven techniques, and 7 actionable activities.

> ✔ Learn how to **DEFY** your limiting beliefs about

yourself and create a life you'll love living.

✔ Be **EMPOWERED** to do more for yourself and demand even more from others.

✔ Learn how to **CHANGE** your self-sabotaging behavior.

✔ Learn how to **RELEASE** fear.

✔ Be **MOVED** by the vivid and transparent personal stories of violent abuse to realize you are not the only one with a past and that it doesn't define your destiny or stop you from getting it.

YOUR FREE GIFTS

As a thank-you for purchasing this book I have created
SIX FREE resources to assist with your personal development:

1. Life Mapping Template

2. Trace Your Life Quick Starter

3. Circle of Influence Infographic

4. Celebrating Self Tip Sheet

5. Personal Budget Planner

6. Spending Journal Sample

Go to the link below to get instant access:

www.ThatAnitaLive.com/bk1

TABLE OF CONTENTS

SECTION I

Chapter One – Dawn of a New Day

Chapter Two – How to Uncover the Happier You

Chapter Three – How to Identify What Has You Stuck and Become Unstoppable

Chapter Four – How to Enforce Your Boundaries

Chapter Five – How to Resolve Fatherless Daughter Pain

Chapter Six – How to Master Your Emotions

Section II

Chapter Seven – How to Make Progress

Chapter Eight – How to Sustain Progress

Chapter Nine – Conclusion

DEDICATION

With all my heart, this work of love is dedicated to The Hill, a country crossroads community with a little red Catholic church and a big blue trailer. You didn't just feed and clothe me, you developed my mind and stretched my soul. You forced me to think, to process thought for the purpose of learning how to do better and consistently become more. You encouraged my dreams. There is a part of me that will always be eight years old enjoying Big Daddy's homemade hand-churned ice cream, Big Mama's parables and proverbs, Cousin Henrietta's corner store, Aunt Pearline's Butterfingers, Aunt Earline's talks as she took in her line-dried, heavenly white sheets, Ms. Thelma's red Kool-Aid, and Cousin Wilhelmina's guiding hand and colorful conversation. Each of you filled me with morals and messages I am still unpacking and from which I am learning my best life lessons. Catholic Hill will always be home.

ACKNOWLEDGMENTS

Thank you God for all your love, protection, guidance, grace, and mercy, for without you, where would I be? And to all of you who have suffered abuse in silence—this is to you.

INTRODUCTION
SUFFERING IN SILENCE

It's 4:20 a.m. My stomach is queasy and I can't sleep. I've been tossing and turning all night. I don't want to go. Do I have to go? Why do I have to go? I hate going. My flight leaves at 10:31 a.m. from National Airport, yet in less than twenty-four hours I've already gone from stressed to frazzled. Who would I have to fight off this time? Whose mistake would I be blamed for this time? How many nights would I end up sleeping in the street this time? What type of wounds would I have to heal this time?

Yesterday I received a voicemail from my aunt. Her voice was shaking. She sounded very distressed, so I called her back immediately. Usually I'd wait until after work. Over the years I've come to know that my family's definition of emergency does not coincide with Webster or the rest of the world—gossip is not an emergency. I called …

"Hello."

"Hey, Auntie O, I got your message?"

"Yes, I'm so happy you called back. Your mom coded blue yesterday. They had to revive her because of an infection in her tubes. You have to come home."

"Okay, um … hold on." Trying to gather my thoughts and make sense of what she said, I asked, "What tube?"

"From the surgery."

"What surgery?"

"Your mom had surgery this week. Didn't she tell you?"

"No, Auntie O. She mentioned a couple of months ago she was having a biopsy done but when I told her I couldn't take off from work for both appointments, she said, 'Well then you don't need to know what the doctor says' and hung up. That was the last I've heard."

"Well, we almost lost her yesterday. You need to come home."

"Auntie O, did she say she wanted me to come home? You know— she *really* doesn't like me the way you all think she does."

"Of course she wants to see you!"

"I think you're responding to *your* feelings and not hearing what I'm saying. I think you should ask her first and be sure."

"I'm sure."

With hesitation and angst I said, "Well, let me see if I can get off work."

My leave request was approved. In fact, my entire office chimed in once they found out my mother was sick. Of course, they had very little clue about the true picture of my abusive and tumultuous family history, but "mother" is one of those titles that gets acclaimed reviews regardless of how she performs in the role. An American mother could sell her nine-year-old daughter into the sex slave trade for a sixteen-ounce bottle of soda and somehow, decades later, after the daughter escapes and creates a better life for herself, America will still say the daughter is indebted to the mother. One coworker said, "Oh 'Nita you have to go, you have to go take care of your mom." Another, "No matter what, you're always supposed to take care of your mom." Another, "I wish I still had my mother."

Until I said, "Yeah—and I wish I'd had your childhood. And have you ever really imagined what '*no matter what*' can include?" A hush fell over the office. I don't do well with family shaming. I never have. People often say, "Family is everything. If you don't have family, you don't have nothing." These people experience emotional and mental blocks when abuse is being inflicted by a family member and attempt to force those blocks onto others. They are causing harm to those of us that are members of abusive families. Their family shaming sends us back into battle zones of emotional and physical war because they refuse to accept a harsh societal reality: sometimes family is not everything.

It's something I wish I could eradicate from the world—people from healthy families, or people putting on a good front that they are from a healthy family, trying to persuade others to live according to their family experience despite what they actually endured in their own. I call it family shaming because I've experienced and witnessed groups of people attempt to use humiliation, critical comments, and the act of singling-out to shame someone into spending time with an emotionally, mentally, or physically abusive family. People family shame for two reasons: 1) they do not have the self-esteem to accept that every story doesn't have a happy ending or 2) they view every situation through the lens of their own pain. Here's an example of number one. As a child Tom was physically abused by an uncle that now lives with Tom's mother. Tom doesn't want to return home for the holidays to spend time at his mother's because every time he sees this uncle, the uncle belittles Tom and attempts to start a fight, which ends with Tom having a black eye or a broken bone again. All while his mother says nothing. However, when learning of his plans not to return home for the holidays, Tom's classmates begin to verbally attack him, trying to make him feel guilty. "Oh my, I can't imagine not spending the holidays with family." "Well, what are you going to do? You can't just be alone for the holidays." "You really should go home; this time could be different." "What if your mom dies between now and next Christmas?" "If you don't go, you'll never know." Tom's classmates are unable to accept the fact that family can be toxic and better left alone. Their refusal to accept Tom's reality is rooted in their refusal to accept their own truth: That they, like many others, turn a blind eye to the dysfunction and abuse in their family. That their family really is not like the Huxtables from the *Cosby Show* or the Cunninghams from *Happy Days*, but a complex and complicated family that makes living life difficult. Why? Because their self-esteem has been beaten into submission until they believe that, whatever someone does to you, if it's family, you just have to take it. Without the self-esteem to value themselves enough to defend themselves, they simply block it out emotionally and refuse to accept abuse exist.

They carve out a fairy tale family they are willing to accept, one that is perfect and comfortable. Here's an example of reason number two. Let's stick with Tom and his dilemma about going home for the holidays, except this time, it's not his classmates but his older coworkers at the post office. "Now, Tom, nobody has a perfect family. You just have to go home for the holidays." "Mama is always right. All that your mother did for you, you know you have to go home for the holidays." Both of his coworkers are parents, speaking from the pain of their own mistakes without knowing any detail about Tom's childhood. They wouldn't want their children to make the same decision as Tom, so they attempt to persuade him not to choose a decision that makes them uncomfortable. Neither of those is a good reason to push a person back into an abusive situation.

I bought a flight home and was now sweating bullets about going. I just couldn't stand it anymore, the fussing and yelling at me about what I couldn't do and who I couldn't be. The attacks to discourage my aspirations. The abuse I'd suffered during my childhood had boiled over and turned into dysfunctional behavior with all its symptoms in my adulthood. The digs and insults at my character, treating me like I didn't matter, trying to fix me by turning me into what they wanted me to be, the fists pounding into my flesh, the kicks—I was sick and tired of being sick and tired of the attacks, the abuse. No matter how many times I proved my mother wrong, I was still never good enough, never worthy of basic respect. No matter how many times I told her what her son had done, I was just expected to be quiet and endure.

THAT WAS THEN, THIS IS NOW

But now I can say that I did finally reach a point where I started to put me first, a time when I began to prioritize my well-being. My level of sick and tired had reached an all-time high. I made the decision not to reset the counter of offenses and pretend it wasn't abuse. I made the decision to stand up for myself and limit access to only those that respected me. It kicked off my exit from the merry-go-round of being abused, then working to heal my physical wounds and repair my emotional health, then being abused again, then working to repair my emotional health again. It led to me having the self-confidence to enforce my boundaries and use my 7-Step Method to become a more emotionally healthy person. In short, I now feel free.

WHAT'S IN IT FOR YOU

In the chapters of this book, I give real-life and in-living-color examples of childhood trauma turning into adult dysfunctional behavior, along with some of the affirmations, techniques, and activities I used to overcome. I demonstrate how you can be told you're nothing, that you don't matter, and how you can be beaten and treated inhumanely every step of the way, but rise and thrive in a beautiful life anyway. Though I was told I could never survive on my own, I've done it. Though they said I wasn't smart enough to get an advanced degree, I've earned two. Every week, consistently, for almost a decade, I heard the same discouraging statement, "You just ought to give up and come home," not because I was going through hard times, but because my family really didn't want me to make something of myself. They wanted me to shrink and accept the submissive, faceless role they were comfortable with because I served as their punching bag and dumping ground. But I didn't, and I'm so much healthier and happier for it. I've taken the knowledge from my Masters of Education in Counseling, my career experience as a counselor, and my personal experience with adult dysfunction from childhood trauma to offer you empowering affirmations, results-driven techniques, and actionable activities to help you minimize their mess, maximize your happiness, and enjoy emotional baggage breakthroughs.

In the stories I share, I give you examples of what could be included in *"no matter what."* I know the battle scars. I know how fear and anxiety can become a part of who you are because of what you've survived. How vulnerability and transparency become the enemy. How we struggle to be humble, with a gentle and quiet spirit, but always have to remain on ready-set-go, prepared for battle with family at any moment.

Sibling abuse, parental neglect, and the witnessing of domestic violence are just a few of the forms of personal abuse I share between these pages. I share them not to cast anyone in a bad light. My hope is this book will do three things: 1) bring awareness to sibling abuse in our society, 2) demonstrate how childhood trauma turns into adult dysfunctional behavior, and 3) move people to take action to heal from their pasts and live their futures in peace and joy.

Chapter One

DAWN OF A NEW DAY

"I dream a world where man no other man will scorn"
"I Dream A World," Langston Hughes

BACK IN THE DAY

Once upon a time, we managed emotional problems with only prayer and encouragement. Seeking professional help was frowned upon. We were taught, *What happens in this house, stays in this house.* Seeking counseling services for divorce or molestation or addiction or domestic violence was taboo. Society expected the wife being battered by her husband to stay married, the niece being molested by an uncle to keep quiet, the daughter with the alcoholic father to make the best of it. Divorce wasn't even regarded as a serious consideration. Instead, any spouse considering divorce was encouraged to make a new commitment to their vows, to pray, and to have faith. We were expected to achieve emotional wellness through a process of suppression and turning a blind eye. Adults had to live their lives according to who they were expected to be and hide who they really were. Children were expected to be seen and not heard.

Remember those days?

The unspoken belief was that when the person died, the problem died with them. When the alcoholic father died, the problems and effects of alcoholism died with him. When the physically abusive mother died, the problems and effects of battery died with her. Unfortunately, nothing could be further from the truth and, because of this, generational curses have been present in our society for centuries. A generational curse is created when the effects of an emotional offense are passed down from one generation to another. It manifests through different dysfunctional behaviors in each family member but can be traced back to one common cause. So how is a

1

generational curse passed down? In emotional baggage.

Children who grow up in dysfunctional environments become adults who exhibit dysfunctional behavior. A child learns from their experiences and from what they're exposed to and then utilizes that later—albeit unknowingly—as a mechanism when they become an adult. In large part, the person you are today is a collection of your past experiences. Your behavior is shaped by what you think, and what you think is determined by what you've seen and heard. Basically, traumatic events experienced during childhood and left unresolved produce dysfunctional behavior in the adult. We carry it around unseen in the form of emotional baggage. Don't believe me? Keep reading. Let me put it in live and living color for you.

THE STORY
THREE GENERATIONS

Imagine a family of three generations: a grandmother, mother, and daughter. Although the grandmother dies a couple years after the granddaughter is born, somehow, at the tender age of sixteen, they will each have become teenage mothers.

The year is 2000. In a small town in the southeastern United States, the high school football team is playing in the state championship game. The entire town is excited. Flat-panel TVs are mounted over the counters of local hotels and fast-food restaurants. Policemen direct the heavy traffic with glow-in-the-dark mascot paw prints painted on the palms of their gloves. Young and old, those with children and those without gather in the local stadium to watch the beloved home team take on their fifty-year rival. The bleachers rock from the beat of the fight songs played by the high school band as the crowd claps and dances along with the cheerleaders. The art club paints paw prints and jersey numbers on the faces of fans of every age. The booster club sells hot dogs, hamburgers, French fries, and popcorn decorated in the team's colors. The junior class volunteers sell commemorative programs and T-shirts to raise money for their impending senior trip. It's the second quarter and the score is 14–7, with the home team in the lead.

While love, happiness, and excitement roar over the bleachers, under the bleachers lives lust and desire. Justin, affectionately called "the Magic Two" by other students, is the son of an alcoholic and the lead-scoring shooting guard for the high school basketball team. He stands six-four, is clean-cut and caramel colored, with hazel eyes. He has set his eyes on Monisha, a 4.0, coke-bottle-curved yet unpopular geek sophomore who has just celebrated her sixteenth birthday—and who is very conflicted. In her head she keeps hearing the one thing her mother has repeated her entire life: "Leave boys alone. They'll ruin your life." But inside she feels the butterflies flutter as Justin says, "You're really beautiful," and wraps his letterman's jacket around her shoulders.

When Monisha was born in 1984, her mother, Monique, was sixteen, and her father, Clayton, was seventeen. They were the head cheerleader and captain of the football team, and everyone adored them. Wherever you saw her, you saw him and his cherry-red Ford Escort. Monique had thick, jet-black, shoulder-length hair and a tiny waist. Clayton had a bright, big, money-grip smile that sparkled with all the promises of possibility for future success. The night of the junior prom, Monique wore a floor-length Carolina Herrera sheath-silhouette evening gown with a twist one-shoulder strap. Clayton was in a black-and-white tuxedo. He picked Monique up at her home at seven o'clock Friday night and dropped her off at noon on Saturday; with that, Monisha was conceived. The generational curse had claimed another member of the family. The emotional baggage of hurt and shame had shut down healthy communication about love, sex, or relationships in Monique's household. Monique too had been the product of a teen pregnancy, a disappointment to not only family but also the community, which was harbored by Millie, Monique's mother, in silence. Millie threw herself into making life look perfect and good, even though she was hurting on the inside. That silence left Monique to learn responsible behavior by trial and error. Millie was too hurt to bring it up for discussion and too ashamed to acknowledge the right way because it would shed light on the fact that she'd done it the wrong way. Millie and Sam, Monique's father, were one of the more well-respected and affluent couples in town, the kind that keeps family faux pas quiet.

In 1968, Millie and Sam were the pride of the local Section 8 project community. A straight-A student, Millie excelled in math and science.

Monique's father, Sam, was the lead singer in a quartet, crooning Motown jams at parties every Saturday night and belting out soul-stirring gospel hymns in the churches every Sunday morning.

Millie and Sam managed to make marriage look good. Millie attended teachers' college and secured a position teaching math at the elementary school. Sam traveled the world extensively, first as a lead singer, then as a solo artist. It was his way of handling his feelings of hurt and shame from teenage pregnancy, creating a family he was not able to provide for. If he didn't see it, he didn't have to face it.

The music hits and the steady paychecks were ever present in Monique's home, but attention and love were not. Her parents provided food, clothing, and shelter but otherwise ignored Monique. She was the evidence of their failure to live a moral life. If they did not look at her, they didn't have to wear the badge of embarrassment. Rumors of Sam's cheating on the road would sometimes filter back to town, but proof didn't materialize until the other wife and children attended his funeral. Neither Millie nor Sam was emotionally present or available to cultivate genuine love in their child. Unconsciously, her parents passed on the emotional baggage of hurt and shame and, though she was always the best-dressed girl in school, the baton of the family curse seamlessly moved from one generation to another and now another.

Monisha, the third generation, has her mother's curves and her grandfather's soulful songbird voice. Her grandmother, Millie, raised her until her untimely death when Monisha was three years old. At that time, Monisha went to live with her mother, Monique, who rarely smiled because, like Monique was to Millie, Monisha was the evidence of the life-altering mistake Monique had made. It had crushed her dreams of attending college and going to law school. She was stuck in a small town working swing shifts at a dead-end hourly job in the local food factory. Her conversations were full of pessimistic snappy comebacks uttered between the cigarettes she chain-smoked. Unfortunately, because of the emotional baggage she carried, she couldn't free herself of the hurt and disappointment so she could mature and be a better mother to Monisha than Millie had been to her. When Monisha entered high school and the house phone started ringing with boys calling, Monique simply hung up the phone and told Monisha, "Leave boys alone, they'll ruin your life." Throughout Monisha's childhood she heard her mother's grumblings about how her father was no good. Monique complained constantly about how Clayton didn't buy food or how he was not trustworthy enough to babysit.

The educational trend of social promotion of star athletes made it very difficult for Clayton to survive at the Ivy League college that heavily recruited him. Though he had a 3.7 GPA, it was obvious Clayton could read and write at only a fourth-grade level, so he dropped out. Out of compassion, the community business owners, who were once high school teammates of Clayton's, employed him for odd jobs until his addiction to alcohol would take over his performance and he would return to rehab to dry out once again. He was of no assistance to Monique.

Teen pregnancy is the epidemic, lack of communication and courage to heal are its enablers, but hurt and shame are the generational curse. And so, two weeks after her sixteenth birthday and just twenty minutes after belting out a soulful rendition of the National Anthem, Monisha is under the bleachers at the state championship football game. She thinks she knows what love is. She believes Justin is the one to give her that forever-after kind of love. Justin has taken her from nerd-weird to crazy-cool with one wink of his eye and made her the most popular girl in school—that's love, or so Monisha feels.

Our biggest problem as a society is that the emotional baggage of hurt, pain, guilt, and shame gets passed down but not resolved. It can live in a family for centuries yet never be discussed openly. Why? Some believe discussing it openly glorifies it. Others believe if it is not discussed, it will go away. These misconceptions breed life into the problem and death to the soul. It forces victims to continue to suffer in silence. It creates a breeding ground for dysfunctional behavior that can hurt future generations.

You've seen it a hundred times. The daughter of a teen mom grows up to have a baby at the exact same age her mom birthed her. The son of a heroin addict grows up to be addicted to heroin. The son of a physically abusive father grows up to physically assault his wife. The daughter of a battered and beaten mom grows up to only feel she is loved—when? When she's being hit. The string of connected dots from one generation to another is a generational curse. But hold on—please do not think the "dots" are always the same kind of dysfunctional behavior.

The pattern of maladaptive behavior can manifest differently in each person. For instance, a father beaten and sodomized in the sixties commits suicide. His son, who was a teen at the time of the incident, becomes a substance abuser. And his son, the third generation, for lack of having a healthy father, becomes a womanizer. Suicide, substance abuse, and womanizing are all dysfunctional behaviors that can be traced back to the experience the family suffered in the sixties. All the behaviors—suicide, substance abuse, and womanizing—are dysfunctional behaviors but not the same behavior. Get it? Maybe this will help …

Imagine three generations of men—a grandfather and his brother, son, and grandson—exhibiting different coping mechanisms but carrying emotional baggage because of the same horrific historic incident.

The year was 1972. MLK Jr. and JFK had been assassinated. On every wall in America hung honors in their memory as the fight for civil rights raged on. Jim and his brother Peter were leaving a protest in Atlanta, Georgia, driving back to Charleston, South Carolina, when they stopped at a country corner store for gas. The sign in the window read "Always Open, All Welcome," but the rifle pushing into Jim's back as he paid for the gas Peter had just pumped said "White's only." Peter was forced behind the store at gunpoint with his hands up in the "don't shoot" position. After the pillowcase went over Jim's head, he began reciting the "Our Father" prayer. He thought about his darling wife, his aging mother, and the murders of Mr. Evers and Dr.

7

King. Jim could hear Peter screaming as he was dragged behind the store. Both men were sodomized, severely beaten, and left for dead. Both men were found by a white college professor returning from a summit in Charleston, South Carolina, to his home in Atlanta when he stopped for gas around midnight and oddly found the store closed.

Jim and Peter were taken to a hospital. When they returned home, they were physically healed but emotionally destroyed. Jim sat for days without uttering a word. His wife continued to love and care for him until his death in 1983, just shy of his son Jeremiah's sixteenth birthday.

Jeremiah doesn't remember his father's happy-go-lucky personality. He remembers only a lump of human existence that sat on the porch from sunup to sundown, and then at the dinner table until bedtime. Because she worked as a housekeeper at the local college, Jeremiah's mother was gone all day, but Jeremiah's Uncle Peter would stop by the house to see his brother, Jim. Somehow, Peter seemed to have bounced back to a normal life—always full of jokes for Jim and candy for Jeremiah. On one particular day, Peter didn't stay on the porch with Jim. He softly walked the house and found it empty, with the exception of Jeremiah, napping in his bedroom. Sitting on the porch, Jim cried as he listened to his son scream for Uncle Peter to stop hurting him, but Jim never moved. Two years later, Jim drove to a nearby pond, locked all the doors on his 1957 Chevy pickup truck, set it ablaze, and burned to death.

Jeremiah's high school friends affectionately called him Jerry. They loved his happy-go-lucky demeanor and warm smile. When they cut class to hang out at the baseball field, he always supplied the booze. Jerry started drinking heavily at fifteen—the same year he fell in love with Susan, the beautiful sixteen-year-old platinum blond with the baby-blue eyes. Together, they smoked, drank, and made love. The next year, they had Justin, a beautiful baby boy with hazel eyes. Jerry and Susan remained a couple. Though Susan worked full-time as a receptionist, Jerry bounced around doing handiwork for the people in town.

In 1984, Justin, a high school sophomore, is the star of the varsity high school basketball team, and Susan could often be seen in the stands sporting a sweatshirt screen printed with Justin's jersey number. His dad, though, never made it to one game. Many nights after he and his mom returned from one of his basketball games, Justin stepped over his father, who was passed out in the doorway. Susan would pick Jerry up and drag him to their bedroom as the phone bounced off the hook, constantly ringing, from a steady stream of girls vying for Justin's attention.

The family curse affected each of the men differently, though the root cause was the same. Peter became a molester; Jim committed suicide; his son, Jerry, became an alcoholic; and his grandson, Justin, was a womanizer. Unresolved guilt, hurt, pain, and shame was the emotional baggage handed down in the family's generational curse. Without a strong positive father figure, the second and third generations were left to deal with the hurt and shame experienced by the first generation and to figure out how to become men on their own.

Everyone has been affected by dysfunctional behavior, if not through their family, then through their job, church, or community. Perhaps you can remember lying awake at night listening to your neighbor abuse his love interest. Maybe you watched over and over as the youth pastor or priest exhibited a stronger interest in one child as they disappeared into rooms alone. Or maybe you've suffered at the hands (or media coverage) of a mass shooter. However you were affected, everyone has some emotional baggage, and they may or may not be properly working through it.

Some people keep their story secret because they've suppressed it so well they aren't immediately aware of it. Others keep it a secret because they think they'd just die if anyone found out. Unfortunately, emotional baggage can cause us to become stuck. It creates insecurities that prohibit us from living our best life in the moment. Insecurities can show up as self-doubt, negative self-talk, low self-esteem, arrogance, conceit, low self-confidence, worry, or indecisiveness.

Behaviors that can become dysfunctional are belittling, intimidating, neglecting, hitting, baiting, threatening, manipulating, lying, choking, abstaining, and indulging.

When we're stuck, the effects aren't always obvious or overt. For example, we've earned two college degrees but still cannot break the desired six-figure income ceiling. We're smart, beautiful, and accomplished but can't find genuine romantic love. We're always around loads of friends and have managed to establish a social calendar that would make Oprah and Gayle blush, but we feel lonely, lost, and purposeless. We're driven, task-oriented, and the highest producer quarter after quarter, but life still feels aimless and empty. We've got the gorgeous husband and brilliant kids, but we feel invisible and underappreciated.

Occurrences are bubbling over, becoming systemic and uncontrollable in homes, schools, and workplaces all over the country. Divorce, addiction, domestic violence, and sexual abuse are social ills that create deep-seated emotional baggage that seeps from the secrecy of our families into mainstream malls, entertainment complexes, and workplaces. Over time they deteriorate the soul of the person carrying the hurt and shame of the trauma, causing that person to inflict wounds on other people. Every problem you have is your responsibility, regardless of who caused it. Take responsibility to not pass your pain to the next generation.

Managing emotional wellness with silence has driven us into a hurricane of destruction on every societal level—from the family to the workplace, church, and school. The bad news is that emotional baggage is killing our communities. The good news is that over the last decade or so, the tide has turned, and emotional wellness is now a societal priority. No longer are we expected to nurse our wounds in silence. It's the best time to find your authentic self and live a fulfilled life of joy. At no other time in history have we had as many life coaches, counselors, and clinicians abundantly available to assist you or corporate brands publicly championing for mental health causes and social responsibility. Now is the time for you to move past the stories that cause you pain. This is your moment. This is your pivotal place in space and time. It is no longer a situation of chance—you get to *decide* to win!

CRACK THE MASK,
BREAK THE MOLD

With this book, I want to help you accept your past and decide it will no longer control your future. I want you to discover the past experiences that created your limiting beliefs and fuel your sabotaging behavior so you can beam with joy from the inside out. I want you to utilize the process of continuous growth and development. Living the same year ninety-nine times is not living a life. There's more, and you can do more than have it—you can thrive in it. I want you to remove the restrictions your past has put on your ability to feel free to live true to your own personality, spirit, and character.

You have to crack the mask to define success and happiness for yourself: In your wildest dreams, what would give you the greatest joy? Think of three things that, if you owned them or earned them, would make you feel like you are living your best life. For example, my three things would be a private jet, a five-acre estate, and a home management staff—no debt. What are your three things? Now, let's do this. Pick up your cell phone (yes, I know it is right there next to you), join my Facebook Group at https://www.ThatAnitaLive.com/group, and post your "Best Life Top 3." We are a safe circle of compassion and understanding. Who knows, your "Best Life Top 3" may pop up in your direct messages when you least expect it as a reminder that dreams do come true—you just have to put in the work.

But understand, time is of the essence. Change is evident and always evolving. Just as times changed to produce a new day of pride in one's authentic self, it can quickly change to make anyone with an emotional issue a dangerous detriment to society. The focus of pop culture and public opinion is largely dependent upon the latest major headline—good or bad. The pendulum swing affects the openness with which we can practice self-help. Today, hashtags that end in "pride" fill every social media timeline daily, but how long will we be able to live unashamed? No one knows, which is why you need to move to create the life you were destined to live now. It's time to soar to your next level in life. Will you continue to go round and round on the merry-go-round of sameness, or will you jump and reach for destiny's brass ring of happiness and success?

IT'S YOUR TIME TO SOAR

In this book, I'm educating, entertaining, and teaching you a new process for dealing with emotional baggage. This process will not only help you to stop living an aimless life but will teach you how to sustain your momentum and steadily accomplish your goals. I'm going to educate you by demonstrating how childhood trauma becomes adult dysfunctional behavior through my own personal stories. I'm going to entertain you with my southern colloquialisms and quick-witted tongue but also by showing you the silver lining to your own dark clouds, the good things that have come out of all those tough times. Lastly, I'm going to teach you how to defend and prioritize what is most important—your happiness and your health.

That new process is my 7-Step Method, which got me off the emotional spin cycle. The basic format of the chapters in Section I are the same. First, I share a personal story highlighting a certain type of abuse and its lasting effects. In some chapters, I give you multiple examples of abusive incidents. I need you to know abusive behavior is not a onetime event. When a survivor says "I was abused," the listener hears and sees one single event. I need you to see, hear, and feel that abuse is repetitive and will persist as long as the perpetrator has access to the victim. Each chapter will also feature a Lesson to Learn section highlighting the dysfunctional behavior resulting from the abuse (the effects), and how the 7-Step Method can be used to overcome the maladaptive behavior (the technique). The activities will teach you how to minimize toxicity, maximize what serves you, and enjoy a meaningful life. Section II of this book—chapters seven, eight, and nine—shares with you how to keep your momentum going once you've gotten free.

The Techniques of the 7-Step Method are:

Step One - Life Mapping
Step Two - Track and Trace
Step Three - Dispose of Distractions
Step Four - Celebrating Self
Step Five - Inner Peace and Quiet
Step Six - Emotional Equation (Performance Review)
Step Seven - Gratitude and Give Back

My successful 7-Step Method Affirmations include:

1. The better I know the person within, the happier I can make her.
2. I am the master of my emotions. I control them, they don't control me.
3. Having boundaries shows I want self-respect. Forcing people to adhere to my boundaries shows I have self-respect.
4. I am precious.
5. I am peace. I am peaceful. I am at peace.
6. I am in a perfecting process.
7. I am receiving goodness and giving greatness back.

My successful 7-Step Method Activities include:

1. Life Mapping
2. Tracking and Tracing
3. Disposing of Distractions
4. Celebrating Self
5. Inner Peace and Quiet (Bonus: Finding My Father Collage)
6. Solving Your Emotional Equation
7. Gratitude and Give Back (Bonus activity: Creating a Family

of Choice)

This book does not include a comprehensive list of all of the Affirmations, Techniques, or Activities in my 7-Step Method. It does include all the steps. However, I've carefully selected the specific Affirmation, Technique, and Activity that best correspond with the lesson to be learned from the True Story in the chapter.

WHY LISTEN TO ME?

I hear you, I hear you. Who is this woman and why should I listen to her? Why should I continue to read this book? Let me give you four reasons: my education, my career experience, my personal experience, and most important—my gift.

I've earned three degrees—a Bachelor of Science in Mathematics, a Master of Education in Counseling, and a Master in Business Administration—and I do mean earned. I attended all my own classes, wrote all my own papers, and conducted all my own research. I learned from professors that cared more for my well-rounded, intellectual development and my ability to rise to the top than my feelings.

But I'm not just heavy on the education side; I'm also qualified by career experience. I've counseled, coached, and trained hundreds of people between the ages of eleven and fifty through their own personal transformations and professional endeavors. I've been a summer teen program counselor and a middle school guidance counselor. I've worked as a counselor in a life skills, education, and technical job training program as well as a career services counselor at a college. And I'm still that one friend everyone seeks out when they need help with their challenges. In addition, as you will learn in later chapters, I've been on every side of emotional baggage.

I am an expert because of the combination of my education, career experience, personal experience, and heavenly gifting at *identifying* where you're stuck and *mapping out* how to move you from where you are to where you want to be in life. Yes, I said "heavenly gifting."

Consider what world-renowned celebrity personality Steve Harvey tells his audiences all over the world about *The Gift*:

> "At birth God gave each and every one of us a gift. A gift is something you do the absolute best, with the least amount of effort. Gifts are more than just running, jumping, singing, and dancing. Your gift is where your success and happiness will be found."

My gift is counseling—picking apart people's insecurities and helping them find their emotional wellness. When life throws everything at you, when you're buried under the mess of this world, I am the hand that you reach for, the hand that will pull you out of the dust, dirt, and mud, then teach you how to live a life of joy, love, and peace.

ARE YOU WITH ME?

Nothing gives you a better understanding of a topic than a 360-degree experience, and as I've said, I've been the victim, the witness, and the conduit God uses to heal.

Using that full panoramic view, I have made this my mission—you will:

- Be **EQUIPPED** to boldly go beyond your comfort zone and refresh, reinvent, and revise your life for the better.
- Learn how to **TRANSFORM** negative thinking into positive thinking with 7 affirmations, 7 results-driven techniques, and 7 actionable activities.
- Learn how to **DEFY** your limiting beliefs about yourself and create a life you'll love living.
- Be **EMPOWERED** to do more for yourself and demand even more from others.
- Learn how to **CHANGE** your self-sabotaging behavior.
- Learn how to **RELEASE** fear.
- Be **MOVED** by the vivid and transparent personal stories of violent abuse to realize you are not the only one with a past and it doesn't define your destiny or stop you from getting it.

In chapter two we'll examine the importance of self-awareness and why no one should know you better than you. We'll review the benefits and the life-changing effects each benefit can have on us. Turn the page, and let's get started.

Chapter Two

HOW TO UNCOVER THE HAPPIER YOU

"Arriving on a nightmare, Praying for a dream"
"On the Pulse of Morning," Maya Angelou

WHY DO I DO THAT?

Unlocking the mystery of who we are and why we do what we do is the master key to moving past your emotional baggage and experiencing a fulfilling and abundant life. Think you completely know yourself already? Let's see how many of the following questions you can answer without hesitation. Go!

1. Why do you live in the geo-area you do versus any other state or country?
2. Why do you prefer tea over coffee or coffee over tea?
3. Why are you strong when others are weak?
4. Why do you (or don't you) fear the police?
5. Why do you like mutton or venison when others do not?
6. Do you cook grits with salt or sugar?
7. Name one of your simple pleasures.
8. What makes you laugh till you cry—deadpan, topical, or satirical humor?
9. What quickly ticks you off the most (only one please)?
10. Name the one event from your past that created the biggest lie you tell yourself?
11. Name your top two pet peeves.
12. What is your most secret fear, something only you know?
13. Name the one event from your past that created your biggest fear?

How many did you answer without hesitation or a second thought?

How many did you stop to think about? If you hesitated on three or fewer, congratulations, you're pretty self-aware. If you hesitated on four to six of the questions, your self-awareness needs improvement. If you hesitated on seven or more, anchor down—your self-awareness needs serious work. These questions all have answers rooted in your history and can help you realize how beliefs and habits form. Even the simple questions have answers that are very telling. Most people prefer tea over coffee or coffee over tea because one or the other was primary in their childhood home. It was a learned behavior. Just like whether you cook grits with salt or sugar or a favorite ageless debate I didn't list, cream of wheat versus grits. This type of self-analysis is a part of the process of becoming more self-aware.

Self-awareness is the master key to unlocking your vulnerability, to being able to face the world unguarded every day and live in a flow of genuine happiness. Self-awareness is the fastest way out of misery. Knowing yourself, your core values, your vision for your life, how you learn, what type of humor you like, and the length of your anger fuse; knowing why you have the dreams, the hopes, and the desires you have—these answers, as well as answers to similar questions, can all be found in the days, weeks, and months we've lived leading up to this very moment. Dr. John Townsend of the *Boundaries* book series posted to Facebook, "People that never ask, 'Now why in the world did I do that?' generally stay stuck in unsuccessful patterns and make others miserable as well." Every time you learn something new about yourself, you move one step closer to your ideal life, one step closer to living unashamed of who you truly are, the authentic you.

Over the next few weeks, I challenge you to tune your ear to listen for the sound of your own laughter. Make a mental (or even a written) note of what you find amusing. Then make a list of the trends and come up with a definition for your own kind of happiness. I also recommend that, if you are part of a couple, you listen for your loved one's laughter and watch for the ever-so-slight romantic blush. Be sure to make that list and hold onto it for all eternity! It'll come in handy during the highs and lows of the relationship.

Both gains and setbacks present challenges. Remember, every blessing comes with an even bigger responsibility, and setbacks come with self-doubt. You must overcome the challenges that come with both to experience emotional baggage breakthroughs. The benefits that come from your growing self-awareness are priceless. But for now, let's take a look at why it's important to know oneself.

IMPORTANCE OF
KNOWING YOURSELF

There are numerous benefits and advantages to being self-aware, to knowing yourself better than anyone else does. Knowing yourself beyond just your likes and dislikes makes moving toward your ideal emotional wellness easier. When you know yourself, you know what motivates you—what drives you. You know your values and what you're willing to sacrifice now, in the process of delayed gratification, so that you can have better later. When you know yourself, you know how you learn; you know how you receive, evaluate, and accept new ideas and information. You know what gives you energy and what drains you of energy. You know what types of people you love to be around, what types of people you can barely stand to be around, and what types of people you will not tolerate being around.

No doubt, your roadmap for happiness and success will have levels, but your movement between levels must be maneuvered carefully. We can no longer view life as a flat line with notches. It must be viewed as a spiral with levels. Because of the rate at which change happens in the world, it is best to remain fluid and flexible, to be ready to adjust at any time because, if you are not moving upward, by default you're going down.

CHALLENGES TO BALANCED
EMOTIONAL HEALTH

All of this knowledge is paramount to maintaining a healthy emotional state of being. You know when your energy is depleted and you need to withdraw to replenish, or when you need to withdraw to be able to give more later. It's a delicate balance to remain emotionally healthy in today's world. We have high crime and low justice. High rates of illness and poor food choices. High taxes with low-quality infrastructure. High cost of living with low salaries. High education costs but low return on investment. All sides of life are pushing pressure down on the little man—me and you. It can be very frustrating and if you are not self-aware those pressures could push you to lose control.

In May 2016, the *Atlantic* magazine published an article titled "The Secret Shame of Middle-Class Americans." The article reported on a statistic from the Federal Reserve Board survey finding that 47 percent of Americans would not have $400 cash for an emergency. They would either have to sell something or borrow the money, or they would not be able to come up with it. This article is proof America is going through a very difficult time, and for survivors of abuse, these external pressures add more challenges to maintaining a healthy emotional state. It further limits their access to resources and benefits that would counter the challenges, making maintaining balance harder.

You don't have to live life so close to the edge. You have to believe that if God allowed you to be exposed to more, then your exposure plays a part in your quest, your diligent seeking, your innermost inhibited desire to obtain it—and becoming more self-aware is your first move. Once you've become self-aware, reaching your goals becomes possible. You know what to change to become the person you admire and dream of being, the person that doesn't care what others think, the person that obtains more, the person that rises to live their best life on the rooftop.

POSITIVE EFFECTS OF
KNOWING YOURSELF

First, stop thinking of yourself as one big collection of all the negative stuff that has happened in your life. Somewhere along the way, some good stuff has happened too, and that good stuff is just as much a part of your story as the negative stuff. The combination of the two creates what I call the unique id of YOU. Your unique id is your beliefs, feelings, and style of relating.

The biggest and most powerful positive effect of being self-aware is the ability to identify and defuse your dysfunctional behavior. Our beliefs are created from our experiences. We think, feel, and behave according to what we believe. Once you know yourself well enough to be able to identify where a certain belief was formed, you are equipped to change your life.

Once you know yourself, you'll be able to lay out a Life Map and link your behaviors and beliefs to the experiences that caused them to form. Understanding these links will help you walk through the rest of the techniques and activities in my 7-Step Method, to evolve into a happier, healthier you. Armed with this information, you have a choice to make: Do you continue your dysfunctional path or do you stretch yourself to disable the old beliefs and adopt practices to form new ones?

I hear almost every day that your happiness and success are outside your comfort zone. That's true. You must learn, grow, and take risks to be successful, but you can't rewire yourself to get there. You must know yourself to chart the right course. Your *wiring* is how you receive and process information and how you generate energy. An abstract thinker cannot become a linear thinker and an introvert cannot become an extrovert for the purpose of being successful.

Here's what I mean. How we consume and process information is our learning style. Most of us are either linear (sometimes referred to as logical) or we are abstract (sometimes referred to as spatial). Linear and logical thinkers process information in terms of related steps, details, and facts; they don't care about emotions. However, spatial and abstract thinkers are emotion driven; they process information in generalizations and scattered patterns. To abstract thinkers, feelings are everything. As for energy styles, introverts generate energy from being alone and extroverts generate energy from interacting with others.

You must know your learning style and energy style to experience the benefits of self-awareness. You are not learning this information to make excuses for yourself, but to know how to perform at your peak and create at your best. If you're learning from an abstract-thinking teacher, you'll know you have to convert the information to best understand it. If you're an introvert and you must attend a series of social events, you'll know you need to plan alone time to recharge between events. Knowing these attributes will help you defuse dysfunctional behavior. Instead of reacting inappropriately, you'll be able to respectfully respond in a calm and rational manner and not feel guilty doing it. You'll be able to create a list of questions to assist you in converting the abstract information so it can be understood by linear minds. You'll be able to give the world a more pleasant and amiable you.

Raising your awareness of yourself will improve your finances and thrust your personal success forward in a way that you've never experienced. Raising your self-awareness helps you know your worth and strengthens your self-esteem. It allows you to decide when to put yourself first, whether or not to keep someone in your life, and how much time and space to give someone in your life. All of these choices and decisions affect your emotional wellness.

Becoming more self-aware through the years has taught me two things. First, if I am going to be around my biological family, I have to also be connected to what I call a "Family of Choice" (FOC). A FOC is a family that is strong and healthy in all the places your family of origin is weak. It is important to balance out your exposure to good and bad. It is important to make a concerted effort to seek out and expose yourself to healthy family structures.

Second, I've learned you can't outrun a family's generational curse. I've traced the curse that flows through my family all the way back to my great-great-grandmother on my maternal side and my grandmother on my paternal side. What's the one common event, you ask? My maternal great-great grandmother had five half-siblings that were all treated much better than she was because they had a wealthy father. My paternal grandmother, who died before I was born, passed from an unknown illness. Her husband, my grandfather, refused a doctor's care and remarried in record time.

Initially I thought my family's generational curse was alcoholism. However, I later learned it is a lack of understanding of emotional hurt, as well as an inability to process it. It is also a lack of understanding of what love is and how to express it. It's one thing to say you know what a watch is; it's another thing to open the watch, exposing all the dials, and say, "I know how a watch works." We all deal with the effects of emotional baggage in different ways. For example, my father was a homicidal alcoholic, my mother lives in the pretty land of "pretend it didn't happen" and "deny it ever did," and my brother uses everything from battery to drunkenness to being completely hollow of emotion. After twenty-five years of prayer and agony, I consciously chose to walk away. We are all dealing with it, in our own way.

Most self-help books give you small snippets or summaries of stories as examples of problems in relation to their solutions. This has always irritated me. To get to know and trust an author, I need the full story—all the details please. In this book, I purposely use my own personal stories, and I give you great detail of my firsthand experiences so you can see specifically how the limiting and untrue beliefs started and the dysfunctional behavior formed. I share great detail because I want you to feel the grave low emotion I felt, but see how it did not overtake my life so you know that, no matter what you've been through, you don't have to allow it to overtake you. I want you to be able to see the connection between the events/trauma and the dysfunctional behavior of my past so that you can begin to draw connections between your past and your behavior. Then you can release the restrictions of limiting beliefs, and look to the future with optimistic expectation.

Even if you are not the intended target, being exposed to abuse can have lasting effects. Here's one of my personal experiences:

TRUE STORY
HIT BUT NOT THE TARGET

I could tell by the tone of my mother's voice on the phone I would not get to finish my homework. "Okay, okay, Dean Williams, I'll be right there. No, no, I understand. Thank you for not calling the police. I just don't know why that boy can't keep his hands to himself."

At this point it had almost become a drill to see how fast I could get all my sixth-grade books and papers up off the kitchen table and into the car. Her next phone call would be to the hospital—calling out of work for the evening, taking vacation time.

I'd complain, "I need to stay home. Why can't I stay home by myself? I got homework to do!"

"Finish it in the car."

I'd walk out the back door, books and papers in hand. She'd lock and close the back door and we'd be off, traveling almost sixty miles through rural areas on backroads in the pitch black dark to my brother's university. She'd flick on the dome light in the car so I could see to do my homework, turning it off when another car approached.

About an hour and a half later we'd arrive to find my brother and sister-in-law's friends and cul-de-sac neighbors standing out in the parking areas, talking. He'd be in a circle of guys off to the side. My sister-in-law would be sitting somewhere holding ice to her face. My mom would fuss, my brother would argue, and my sister-in-law would cry. Sometimes I went in and finished my homework on their apartment floor. Other times I just used my books for a pillow, lay down in the backseat of my mother's chocolate-brown Chevrolet, and went to sleep, knowing in the next few days, we'd *all* do this *all* over again.

To my recollection, this tumultuous couple always fought. From the first time I met his then-girlfriend, I remember them having violent arguments and fights. I remember seeing him push her down the stairs. I remember her being pregnant and having a black eye. I saw three different law enforcement agencies in three different jurisdictions tell my brother to take a walk around the block and cool off as my sister-in-law bandaged her wounds. I remember eavesdropping on a conversation between my brother and a family friend, a well-respected teacher and athletics coach, as they sat on my mother's porch and my brother fiddled with a black contractor-sized garbage bag filled with all his earthly belongings. Coach was telling my brother it's wrong to hit. My brother was telling Coach that he and his wife would reconcile because he stilled loved her. They were each having a one-way conversation: everything Coach said fell on deaf ears.

Even though I was not the one physically assaulted or the one being verbally attacked, both my pursuit of high scholastic achievement and my tenacity to always complete my homework dropped off significantly. My respect for my sibling vanished. Though I wasn't being directly hit, punched, or kicked, the emotional ramifications were almost the same.

LESSON TO LEARN

The lesson to learn here is that childhood trauma has immediate and long-term negative effects. In this case, witnessing domestic violence led to the immediate negative effect of lackadaisical academic achievement and the long-term effect of withdrawal from family. Though at the beginning of the year I tested in the top percentile of my class, my grades began to drop, and the feeling that all I needed to do was pass was born. Once my brother's battery took center stage, my homework was no longer important. As a ten-year-old I learned high academic achievement wasn't a priority. It lasted until graduate school.

Children learn from what their parents do, not from what they say. Younger hearts and minds are always watching. Your behavior today is shaping the lessons they learn and the behavior they will exhibit tomorrow. Make time for what you want children to know is important.

Along with my grades dropping, I began to skip as much family time as I could. I kept my thoughts and opinions to myself. I withdrew not just physically, but also verbally, because watching violence hurt, even when I wasn't the target. Witnessing the fights between my brother and his wife, and my brother and my mother, made me feel hopeless. I felt incapable of helping my sister-in-law and defeated by watching him yell at and push our mother. As I grew older, I joined school sports teams and other extracurricular activities just to be away from the house. As more trauma occurred, my withdrawal from family increased. I endured this situation in silence until college gave me an out. Eventually, the limiting belief I learned was that women are only respected by men outside their homes.

Now, ask yourself, are you a person you would think highly of? If the children in your life right now grow up to do the things they see you do, would you be proud? Even though they may not see you do it, they may still be able to tell. Even when I had not seen my brother beat his wife, when he came busting through the door panting and yelling, I knew he had been fighting someone, and more than likely it was her. Every time you expose a child to danger, you shape their future and diminish their chance of being a well-adjusted and happy adult. You create a situation that manifests chaos and crime in our communities. Now that you know better, I challenge you to do better.

If any of this chapter resonates with you, I beg you to start the journey to overcome the control your past has on your present and future, now. It requires commitment and dedication to stay on course to healing but do it, for you, for me, and for the safety and health of our community.

Three other events in my life that led to me becoming more withdrawn from family but also more self-aware were my father's attempts to burn down our home. Yes, he made three different attempts. Though they happened early in my life, their impact on my self-awareness didn't come until much later. I didn't know my own strength. I didn't know I could act for safety first and react to disbelief second. His first attempt is more of a memory than an experience because I was a mere toddler, but the second and the third clearly shaped my thinking and future interactions with my family. More on how it led to me becoming more self-aware later. For now, the story.

TRUE STORY
HOUSE FIRES

THE FIRST TIME

I was a toddler, asleep in my crib. I felt someone jerk me up and carry me away. When I opened my eyes, I was outside. There we sat on the cement block steps on the front of the house under the porch light. It was dark out. It was still. Nobody was outside playing. No cars were driving by. It was peaceful. But there was a smell in the air—an unfamiliar smell. Then I saw smoke in the air.

I remember seeing the screen door swing open and shut as my brother ran back inside to help our mother put out the fire, but she sent him back to the porch. As the screen door swung open and closed, I could see my mother rush between the kitchen and the den with a pitcher or a pot of water. I knew I wasn't smelling cigarette smoke. It wasn't smoke from a wood-burning fireplace. It didn't smell like tree-burning smoke, the kind that drifts when clearing the land after a timber cutting. This smoke smell was different. To this day, I still have difficulty describing it. We sat there on the front steps for what seemed like hours. Then I was put back to bed.

Turns out, my father had set the sofa on fire, trying to burn down the house where his wife and kids lay sleeping. Though I was very young, I remember thinking, "Did my father try to kill us?" As a teen, I would come face-to-face with the hard but true answer to that question.

Many times during my childhood, when I was alone in the den, I would turn up the upholstery skirt on the couch and look at the

37

burned wood underneath, mentally recreating the scene, piecing together what I remembered with all the doubtful versions I had heard from my mother and brother over the years. Trying to see if the smell of the burned wood matched the one etched in my memory. Trying to figure out why someone would set something on fire to harm those who were supposed to be their loved ones.

I'd torture myself wondering—how could a cigarette drop from someone's hand and roll across the throw rug and onto the vinyl floor under the sofa? If he was asleep on the sofa, and the cigarette was in an ashtray, wouldn't the top of the sofa burn first? Wouldn't the throw rug have burned? If he was asleep on the sofa, why did the smoke wake up everyone but him? When he woke up, he would have come to check on his kids, right?

For years my mom and brother called this event "an accident," denying my father ever tried to cause anyone harm. I've heard various versions of how our father fell asleep and somehow managed to accidently set the sofa on fire, that he was not at all trying to burn down the house. However, as I got older and he tried again and again, it became undeniable.

THE SECOND TIME

I was in high school. My mother was asleep in the front bedroom, and I was lying on the sofa watching television in the den, laughing hysterically. JJ and Thelma of the television show *Good Times* were arguing over the bathroom for the hundredth time and then—there was that scent again.

I tried with all my might to compare it to every smell I could think of, but I couldn't figure out what it was. I couldn't identify it. I knew it wasn't a potbelly stove because my grandmother had one of those, and it didn't smell like that. I knew it wasn't a wood-burning fireplace because one of our neighbors had one of those, and it didn't smell like that. This smell was distinct because in some way it smelled familiar.

I was sure I'd smelled it before but I just couldn't think of where or when—until it brought back an earlier memory.

My heart sank into my stomach as a jackhammer pounded in my chest. I couldn't breathe. No matter how hard I tried, my lungs were locked and not taking in air. I saw flashbacks of sitting on the porch in the dark. Flashbacks of my mother hurrying between the kitchen and the den with a pot of water. Flashbacks of burned wood under sofa upholstery.

I jumped up off the sofa and ran past the deep freezer into the kitchen to the back door. I could see him through the screen door, and a burning rage raced up through my legs and back. My blood boiled and burned, circulating through my body like kerosene singeing my soul one inch at a time. My arms hung like dead weight, and my mouth dropped open even as my adrenaline started rushing. Fueled by anger, I felt painful knots tightening in my shoulders. He was standing there pressing burning, twisted newspaper against the house, trying to set it ablaze.

It took everything I had, but I resisted the urge to punch him in his face and stomp him to the ground. Instead, I ran to the side of the house and grabbed the water hose. The faucet knob was so tight I couldn't get it to turn. I kicked it but it still didn't move. I had to get down on my knees and press my body weight into the faucet to finally get it to loosen. Running back to the corner of the house where he was still holding the burning newspaper, I soaked everything—the newspaper, the house, and him.

I finally felt air fill my lungs to capacity and then deflate like a balloon. I was exhausted. As I tried and failed to catch my breath, I waited for him to make the first move. I wanted a fight. I wanted a knockdown, drag-out, pound-his-face-into-the-pavement-until-he-pissed-tar fight. But he didn't say anything. He didn't even look at me. He walked past me, out of the yard, and up the street, back toward the liquor stores.

Blessedly, I had caught him before he caught the house. There wasn't any damage to the house, but my soul and belief in family were changed forever.

Just then, my mother appeared in the screen door and asked why I didn't just come get her. Silly me, I thought I had my priorities in order. I thought catching a small fire came before waking her up and announcing we had a big fire.

She went back to bed, and I went back to Thelma and JJ ... like nothing ever happened.

THE THIRD TIME

It was a fabulous day. A perfect day for a teenager to be at the neighborhood park. Humidity was low, the heat was mild, and the park was packed! The swings were full, and kids were busy playing in the tot area. Music was humming from the cars as some of the guys waxed their paint jobs while others played full-court basketball. Everyone else was sitting on the sideline benches, laughing and talking about teachers, homework, and our eighth bus driver of the year quitting. It was great until I heard someone yelling my name.

He was running toward the court from the dirt-road side street. "The fire truck is at your house! The fire truck is at your house!" My other friends asked if I wanted them to come. "Nah, I got it."

I jogged back toward the house with my friend who had come to get me. From the top of the hill, I could see the smoke rising in the sky. As I approached the house, the fire truck was pulling off. I walked up the driveway and saw my mother standing in the corner of the backyard with the water hose in her hand, water still dripping from the nozzle. This time he had actually managed to catch the house on fire—a big black burned spot covered the boards under the den windows and stretched from the end of the house to the back door. He was nowhere in sight.

Why didn't she call the police and have him charged with attempted murder? Why was he still walking free when this was his third attempt? Why did my mother continue to accept these attempts on our lives?

In his song "Let It Go," Kirk Franklin said it best, "Take it serious, the demons in a man's mind." You can't live a healthy life in a toxic relationship. You have to be intentional about creating an environment where you can grow and prosper. If you're raising children, you are a protector. Take serious the responsibility God has entrusted you with. You are lighting powerhouses to send out into society, and what you send affects the future of the world—the rate of crime, poverty, education, and wealth depends on your actions as a parent.

Hopefully it is easy for you to see how the limiting beliefs I had originated. A child depends on their parents for protection. However, the first man in my life attempted to end my life three times before I reached the age of sixteen.

So many parents, much like my own, have ignored the dysfunction in their families at the expense of their children. Molestation, physical violence, alcoholism, cocaine addiction, even favoritism between children can turn a loving, healthy child into a toxic adult, an adult that will one day be someone's boss, father, mother, or coach. If you had a similar experience with your parents, what limiting beliefs did it create for you? How have you worked to overcome them? If you haven't, now is a good time to start.

If you have children, take time to observe them. Get to know your children and love them enough to protect them. The cycle of denial and pretend breeds enablement, and enablement fuels the cycle of dysfunction.

LESSON TO LEARN

The lesson to learn here is (*have I said it enough*) childhood trauma becomes adult dysfunctional behavior. Being exposed to my brother's battering (domestic violence) and surviving my father's homicidal attempts developed a self-protective guard of keeping people at a distance and formed more limiting beliefs that lasted for the better part of twenty years: never trust anyone to protect you; learn to do for yourself and to take care of yourself.

Learning how to protect yourself and do for yourself could be construed as good attributes. But when they are motivated by limiting beliefs that were formed by violence, the effect is negative, not positive. Here's how…

Remember reading in my ebook, *7 Simple Steps to Beat Emotional Baggage*, about the iron case around my emotions? (If you haven't read my ebook, it's a free download at ThatAnitaLive.com/ebook) Well, this is how it formed. I had to have my guard up at all times. Each additional violent event added another layer of iron. Being iron tough may sound good in a mafia movie, but in real life, it's dysfunctional. We should be open and healthy enough to live true to ourselves. We're blessed through people. We experience the fullness of life with people. I've come to know that the healthy thing to do is to learn to discern the wheat from the tare by the fruit they produce. Which is where the saying, "Once people show you who they are, believe them" comes from. It teaches us that once we realize we are dealing with tare, with people that do whatever they want at the expense of others, we should stop looking for the good in them, stop trying to force them to be something they are not. The fruit they produce is their actions. Unethical, immoral, illegal, or even selfish behavior is bad fruit.

What kind of fruit do you produce? Are you a person that has a conversation with someone for the purpose of regurgitating everything they shared with you to someone else? Is that good fruit? Are you a person that hides their hurt under the dysfunctional behavior of so-called "keeping it real"? If so, I hope you can be honest with yourself and mature. Maturing includes healing from your past. It may require you to change your environment, your friends, and your circle of influence. Start with your mindset and keep going.

Later in chapter four you'll see very clearly how my being dismissive and overly passive about the emotional abuse I was enduring led to a very disturbing and frightening experience.

7-STEP
METHOD AFFIRMATION

The better I know the person within, the happier I can make her.

This revelation came to me in graduate school. I observed that the longer I wasn't exposed to my bio-family, the happier I became. I began to notice a trend, a roller-coaster effect of low-high-low. My lows were phone calls and visits with them. My highs were all the time I spent away from them. I noticed that before every phone call and visit, I would repeat mantras that celebrated my positive qualities and recent accomplishments. After every phone call and visit, I matched the insults, the belittling, and the punches to the "before" mantras and disempowered the negative effects of the continuing abuse. This realization became a part of the foundation of the techniques and affirmations I built to fight for myself and my own kind of happiness. I hope it strengthens and helps to build a more resilient you.

I often like to compare our emotional development to my grandma's garden. Every year at the start of planting season, my grandfather would walk the land. Though it appeared he was just wandering around with his hands in his pockets, he was actually familiarizing himself with whatever debris the storms had washed into the garden. He was preparing the land to become a healthy place for growth. Before any seed could be planted, the land had to be cleared of all the rocks, weeds, and paper that would prevent the process. It's the same with us. We must familiarize ourselves with whatever is already present—beliefs, feelings, and behaviors. Before we can begin the process of becoming emotionally healthy, we have to take account of what is already present that could impede or prevent the process of healing and growth from occurring. We must become more self-aware.

Becoming self-aware will empower you to realize your priceless value and will lift loads of worry and stress off your shoulders. Your personal flow of authenticity and creativity will start to spring out of you. Out of your flow will come contentment and happiness. Out of your flow will come satisfaction with yourself. Out of your flow will not only come your dreams, but also the belief, the self-confidence that you can achieve them.

7-STEP METHOD TECHNIQUE
LIFE MAPPING

To begin your journey of becoming more self-aware, start with Step One of my 7-Step Method, which is Life Mapping. I call it Life Mapping because it enables you to see the terrain of your life: the highs, lows, rough patches, serene beaches, and rocky regions. It's the process of walking back through time and documenting the events that have happened throughout your lifetime. This step helps you to identify the experiences in your life that have had lasting impact. It helps you to identify the occurrences in your life that have created the person you are today. It's a discovery period for you to relax and remember. This technique simply has you write down everything that could possibly be a "cause." A cause for why you have difficulty trusting people. A cause for why you have poor spending habits. You are not linking causes with effects. You are not asking yourself why you do certain things. You are just remembering at this point. You are just recalling and listing the events that have happened. You may have to take some time and concentrate to bring back deeply suppressed memories, but you must be completely honest and transparent to achieve the full benefit of this step.

7-STEP METHOD ACTIVITY
LIFE MAPPING

To complete this activity, think of your life in stages. You can use age groups, school grades, and addresses to break it down. Take time to think over each stage and write down any life events that occurred during that stage. If you feel worksheets would help guide you better, you can create your own or download the Book Bonus Gifts, which includes a Life Mapping Template (LMT). Go to ThatAnitaLive.com/bk1 to download your gifts today. If you prefer to create your own, here's how. You're going to create a table of triggers using your age as a guide. Start with ten or so sheets of paper. Use one sheet of paper to create one table for each of the following age groups: 0-5, 6-9, 10-13, 14-18, 19-22, 23-30, 31-35, 36-40, 41-45, 46-50 and so on. Your rows will be your age and the columns will be titled school grade, home address, life events, and hobbies/extracurricular activities. So, on your first sheet of paper, you would number the rows 0, 1, 2, 3, 4, and 5 to represent your ages during this stage. In the second column, write the daycare or school grade associated with the age in each row. In the third column, write the home address that corresponds to the age and grade in the previous two columns. Starting to see the pattern? In the remaining columns you will write the life events and hobbies associated with the previous columns. On the bottom half of each sheet of paper you will write any experiences and memories you remember. You will complete this exercise for every stage of your life. It's probably a lot simpler to download the templates I've created for you. Here's the web address again, ThatAnitaLive.com/bk1.

COMING UP NEXT

In the next chapter we'll look at how nightmares and anxiety in adulthood are by-products of childhood trauma and how sibling abuse is a real issue. It is not the same as sibling rivalry, which can be very healthy if suitably managed by the parents. Sibling abuse is cruel and violent. It has harmful effects that can fuel dysfunctional behavior for a lifetime if not addressed and resolved. This is why it is so important to uncover the events in your life that have had the biggest impact on your inability to reach your pinnacle of happiness and to attain contentment with your life.

Notice I continue to use the term "contentment." It's intentional. Many would have you believe you are to live your life going from one motivational high to another, that if you are not living in a constant state of euphoria, you are clinically depressed and require medication. It's simply not true. In life you will experience highs and lows, but most of your time will be spent in the middle, in a place called "contentment," a place where you just feel good.

Chapter Three

HOW TO IDENTIFY WHAT HAS YOU STUCK AND BECOME UNSTOPPABLE

"How I long for something better than this life I know too well.
Lord, I know I'm bound for heaven, 'cause I've done my time in hell."
"Children of the Night," Richard Marx

STUCK AT THE WINDOW

Thousands of women all over the world feel stuck at the window. They feel their life is stagnant, but through the window they see other people enjoying magnificent lives. They secretly have goals and dreams, things they would like to do and accomplish but, year after year, they are no closer to those dreams than they were a decade ago. Even if they make an attempt to move forward in life, the move doesn't feel fulfilling. It feels more like one daunting step on an impossible journey. Is this you? Well, get out of the window and in front of the mirror. There in the mirror is everything that will transform your life. Remember, it doesn't matter who caused the problem in your life, it is your problem to solve. Most of us don't realize how much our past is holding us back from experiencing a better future. We hold on to our past through the limiting beliefs they created. Your limiting beliefs are untrue and within those untrue beliefs are statements that affect the way we see ourselves, what we are capable of and not capable of, the way we feel about ourselves. All of those suppressed statements and deep-seated feelings affect how we go after the life we really want to live—aggressively, believing we can obtain it, or from a distance, never really committing to get it done.

IS YOUR PAST YOUR GLASS CEILING?

One of the types of abuse that plays a significant role in my life is sibling abuse. As of this writing, I am enduring stalking and harassment from my brother, all for the sake of control and domination. It amazes me how easily some people allow themselves to be manipulated into assisting with abuse. Let me make this practical. My family says to you, "Oh, we're just checking to see if she's ok, we just want to know if she's still breathing." You as the spectator think to yourself, "That's so sweet. She shouldn't ignore her mother and her brother like that." You divulge my location. My family arrives, puts a plastic bag over my head, and ties it around my neck—to see if I'm still breathing of course. You, the spectator, assisted them, but I'm the one feeling the effect of their actions. I'm the one suffocating.

A lot of people snicker and laugh when the subject of sibling abuse is discussed because they dismiss it as sibling rivalry, but after forty years of suffering, I can tell you it is no laughing matter.

I am going to use sibling abuse and parental neglect as my examples of how to discover what has you stuck and how to become unstoppable. Because sibling abuse isn't as well known and researched as domestic violence, let's clarify exactly what it is and discuss its place in society.

WHAT IS SIBLING ABUSE?

Sibling abuse is a form of family violence largely ignored and dismissed as harmless sibling rivalry. Parents, schools, even psychology experts say it's hard to tell the difference between sibling rivalry and sibling abuse. Reasons credited for the difficulty include the following facts: "No specific federal law protects siblings from other siblings, a standardized clinical definition does not exist and mandated reporters such as teachers, counselors, therapists, social workers and coaches have not been trained in how to detect, identify or treat sibling abuse." (Meyers, 2015). I believe these facts, in addition to the reluctance of parents to publicly admit violence happens in their home, contribute to the normalization of sibling abuse and reinforce the community norm that victims have no voice. I find it really hard to believe any form of abuse is unrecognizable over the long term.

Merriam-Webster defines abuse as: "Treating a person or an animal with cruelty or violence, especially regularly or repeatedly, and speaking to or about someone in an insulting and offensive way." Why does the definition of abuse become cloudy when the application is moved from a husband/wife relationship to a brother/sister relationship? Why does the definition become cloudy when the application is moved from two classmates in school to two siblings at home? Kiselica and Morrill-Richards (2007), through a review of over fifty research studies, were able to identify psychological (mental and emotional) abuse as words and actions that express contempt and degradation such as belittling, intimidation, and provocation, and physical abuse as one sibling causing deliberate physical harm to the other, such as kicking, biting, suffocating, and punching. Are you with me so far? Merriam-Webster's definitions match those of Kiselica and Morrill-Richards. It doesn't matter if the verbal outburst or physical kicking is being committed by a sibling or a husband, by a classmate or a parent—abuse is abuse.

Caffaro & Conn-Caffaro (2005) have deduced a definition for sibling abuse from their independent research studies dating back to 1998, "Sibling assault can be defined as a repeated pattern of aggression directed toward a sibling with the intent to inflict harm, and motivated by an internal emotional need for power and control." Meyers' (2015) has defined it as abuse that includes unpredictable and relentless acts of intimidation resulting in a state of helplessness and isolation.

Still, parents report that it is hard to tell the difference between two siblings that are participating in rivalry and a situation where one sibling is inflicting abuse on another. However, Kiselica and Morrill-Richards, in their review, were able to deduce, "Normal sibling conflict usually consists of a mutual disagreement over resources in the family (e.g., parental attention), whereas sibling maltreatment consists of one sibling taking on the role of aggressor in relation to another sibling." Specifically, social work researcher and Molloy College professor Amy Meyers cited the importance of the reciprocal element that differentiates sibling rivalry from sibling abuse, where each child has equal opportunity to win (Meyers, 2015).

Still, let's take an even more granular look at one form of sibling abuse, bullying. A research study of sibling pairs conducted by Skinner and Kowalski (2013) of Clemson University examined sibling bullying occurrence rates and the extent to which siblings perceive sibling bullying to be normal. The research participants were sibling pairs, age eighteen and older. Here are a few of their findings:

- 78% of respondents reported being bullied by their sibling
- 83% of victims reported the most common method as being verbally teased in a hurtful way

- 69% of victims reported the second most common method as being physically bullied (e.g., hit or kicked)
- 66% of victims reported the third most common method as being excluded or ignored
- 26% of victims reported the bullying lasted more than several years
- Another 7.5% reported that bullying was still going on
- 55% of victims reported their mother, father, or both were present when the bullying occurred

Dysfunction in our homes, schools, churches, and work environments is rampant and requires not only prevention strategies but also commitment from parents, corporate management, and mandated reporters to change behaviors they are modeling, whether through omission or commission. There comes a time when silence is condoning and condoning becomes betrayal. But let's take a more personal and in-depth look at examples of my own sibling abuse, inflicted by my brother who was ten years older than me.

TRUE STORY
MY BROTHER THE BATTERER

My mother always says she noticed a drastic change in my personality when I was about thirteen. To that I say, of course she did. When you're thrown into situations where you don't have anyone to protect you, you learn to speak up for yourself, however it comes out. I have countless memories of interactions with my sibling, but not one of them is positive. Nor can I remember our mother ever saying anything disapproving of my brother's abusive behavior.

There's the time my mother, brother, and I were sitting in Morrison's Cafeteria when I was about ten years old. As every time before, I gave my mother my order for her to approve or disapprove and relay the final choice to the waitress. However, this time, my brother decided it was time for me to begin ordering my own food. He chastised our mother and told her under no circumstance was she to order on my behalf, that if I didn't order, I didn't eat.

The waitress came, took my brother's and our mother's order, and then turned to me. "And for you sweetie, what'll you have?" I couldn't talk. I choked on the words. I felt so meaningless and insignificant. One by one, the tears began to roll down my face. My brother excused the waitress from the table. "I guess she won't be eating."

The food came. Our mother ate. My brother ate. Our mother paid the bill and we left the restaurant. Our mother never said a word. An hour later, arriving home, I ran to a neighbor's house for food, comfort, and understanding.

There's the time I was on the phone chatting with a school classmate. (You remember that phone, don't you? Back before call waiting, cell phones, and tablets existed. Back when homes only had one phone in the entire house, the rotary dial phone in the kitchen on the wall.) I was about thirteen years old, sitting in a chair at the kitchen table, when my brother stomped around the corner from the den into the kitchen, snatched the phone out of my hand, slammed it down on the hook, and marched back into the den. I dialed the call back, briefly explained what had happened, and began the conversation again.

About five minutes later, here my brother came, and again he snatched the phone out of my hand and slammed it down on the hook, but this time he yelled, "And don't get back on it." I asked if he needed to use the phone, and he yelled no. I asked if he was waiting for a phone call, and he screamed no. I picked up the receiver to once again restart my conversation, but he tried to take the receiver away from me. A tussle ensued.

He grabbed my throat and began to squeeze. I remember thinking, *Not this time. He will not choke me until I pass out and then discard my body into my bedroom like trash. I matter.* I grabbed a knife from the stove but felt a pull on my hand refusing to let me cut his arm. That force was our mother. She shouted, "Well, just stay off the phone!" I ran out the back door, silently counting the years and months to high school graduation, and my freedom.

I have many memories but none of them had the rippling and lasting effect this next one did. I remember it vividly—the cool, crisp midnight air slammed against my face and stung my lungs. My side began to burn. The faster I ran, the more I lost my breath. I felt nauseous and started getting lightheaded. All I knew was that I had to get away. I didn't know where to go, but I knew I had no one I could trust. Runaways got dragged back to the home. No one ever asked what you were running away from. All I could think was, *Run.*

I was about fifteen years old and finally allowed to stay home by myself when my mother worked nights. I enjoyed being able to rest in the quiet, without the yelling, fighting, or screaming of my parents or sibling. I enjoyed being able to watch TV without someone walking in and changing the channel in the middle of the show I was watching. I enjoyed being able to chat on the phone and not have anyone snatch it from my hand and hang it up midsentence.

At this time my brother was twenty-five years old and had moved out and on with his life—well, he'd moved out but not on with his life. He'd moved in with a girlfriend across town. They'd drink alcohol and fight, and somehow, time after time, the fighting would spill over onto me at our mother's home. This particular night, I was lying on the sofa in the den watching TV. He rushed into the house, slammed the back door shut, and blew into the den, panting and breathless. He slammed his hand against the power button on the TV, turning it off, then grabbed me up off the sofa, threw me onto the floor, and laid on the sofa himself. He reeked of alcohol.

He yelled, "Go to bed." I got up off the floor, turned the TV back on, and sat in the rocking chair. He rushed the TV, punching the power button and almost pushing it completely off the stand, then he grabbed me out of the rocking chair. I swung and kicked as hard and as many times as I could, but nothing seemed to help. I couldn't get loose. A decade older and twice my height and weight, he dragged me across the den floor and threw me into the dining room. My head hit the hardwood floor.

I was tired of being pushed to the sidelines for the convenience of her son. I was sick of being treated like an object and not a human being. I hated being a member of this family. I couldn't wait to graduate high school, leave, and never return. I knew I had a right to watch TV in a house I was supposed to call home. I knew I was being mistreated. I knew I had to fight.

Once again, I got up, went back to the TV, and pushed the power button. Suddenly, I felt a dull blunt pain in the back of my head. I remember all the strength draining from my body as I went limp and dropped to the floor. My vision went blurry, then black. I got up off the floor and stumbled through the dining room, then the living room, and out the front door.

The fresh air helped me see my way through the dark. Everything was blurry but I made it off the porch, down the sidewalk, and into the street. I started running. I reached the top of the hill but I knew I couldn't stop there. My side burned, the air was thin, I couldn't catch my breath, but I kept running. I needed to sit down, but I couldn't stop. I knew I couldn't stop running and I couldn't go back. But where could I go?

I leaned against the flag pole in front of the school as a tingling sensation ran up and down my legs. Unable to stand I dropped to my knees and lay down in the grass, my head pounding. My chest felt full and tightened with every breath I tried to take. I knew my mother wouldn't be home for at least another eight hours. Where could I rest until then? Where would I be safe?

I heard a car approaching and hurriedly crawled to hide behind the school sign. I saw the headlights, but made it behind the sign without the driver seeing me. The last thing I needed was a neighbor to force me to return home or a stranger to do worse. It rounded the curve heading toward the neighborhood and kept going. After that close call, I knew I couldn't stay there.

Using the bricks in the school sign to pull myself up, I managed to stand. Once I was on my feet, I stumbled to the side of the school and fell asleep on the heating grate behind the cafeteria. The next thing I felt was warmth from the sun. It was morning.

Slowly, I started the walk back to the house, wondering, "God, why was I born into such a hostile family? Why are these people so violent and hateful?" As I walked into the driveway, every step I took felt like I was sinking deeper and deeper into the sand, making it hard to go back into the house. The air got thick. It was hard to breathe. I turned the key in the door. As I stepped through the kitchen, I heard only silence. No one was home. I got into bed fully clothed and fell asleep.

That afternoon when I woke up, I sat in the kitchen and waited for my mother to get off the phone. I tried to tell her, "Ma, he came back here last night and was punching me."

An argument ensued.

"Well, why didn't you just go to bed?"

"I don't have a right to watch TV in this house?"

"Well, that's just your brother, that's how he is."

"So, I don't matter? No matter what he does, he's right?"

She turned her back to me and started singing and stirring a pot on the stove, as if I wasn't even standing there. *God, I can't wait to get away from here.*

I slammed my bedroom door shut, hit the power button on the radio, and turned the volume up so I could feel the beat of the music vibrating in my soul, relieving the pain. Shouting the words as Bon Jovi sang "Dead or Alive" relieved some of the tightness in my chest and arms. I daydreamed about having peace in my own house, about boarding my own steel horse and never having to deal with this family again. One day, I knew I would be free.

AGAIN

A month or so later, in the darkness of the night as I slept in my bedroom, one by one, over and over I felt the blows rain down on my back, neck, and head. I couldn't lift my head to see whose fists were pounding on me or who was pushing me back down. I managed to curl my knees into my chest before he lifted me up and threw me to the floor. Through the glare of the light that poured in from the hallway, I could see the hatred in my brother's eyes. As I tried to crawl into the hallway and then the dining room, he kicked me in my side.

Once I made it to my feet, I ran through the living room to the front door and felt the cold air burn my throat as I leaped off the porch onto the sidewalk, then from the sidewalk to the street. The only sound I could hear was the ringing in my ears. All the neighbors' homes were dark, but the vision was so real I could touch it. In my mind I could see the heating grate at the school.

Still running, I smelled the smoke from one neighbor's fireplace as I passed the intersection. The burn in my legs and my back said, "Stop running," but the tears running down my face said, "Hit the interstate and hitchhike, hurry! Get someplace else." I was so torn. I never wanted to go back but I knew that teens weren't listened to or valued; they were simply and directly returned to sender. Besides, if no one listened to me when I was five or six and cried every day of first and second grade, why would they listen to me now? Where would I hitchhike to?

Arriving at the school, I sat on the grate and took deep breaths. No matter how deep the breath, my heart raced at lightning speed and showed no signs of slowing down. I squeezed my fingers together, trying to stop my hands from shaking. Finally, I just lay back on the heating grate. My chest burned even more but, because of the weakness in my arms and legs, I couldn't sit up. I rolled left. I rolled right. But I couldn't sit up. I closed my eyes. What seemed like only an hour later, there it was again—the warmth from the morning sun.

This went on for almost a year. No matter how many times I told my mother, she either ignored me or defended her son. More and more I began to pray to go to college and never see any member of this family again. I began asking God to release me from the obligation of spending time with family or "honoring thy mother and father." I made my decision. I had only to wait for high school graduation.

DYSFUNCTION BEGETS DANGEROUS BEHAVIOR

"College! I'm finally free!"—or so I thought. High school graduation was behind me. I was moved into the dorm and my family was gone. Whew! Yaaasss! I was so elated to be away from that house and those people. I felt safe. I felt secure. Though the emotional, mental, and physical abuse had finally stopped, the residual effects lived on long after the experiences.

Most of us tend to think that when the damaging behavior stops, the entire ordeal is over. When related reactions and symptoms occur later, they get displaced or attributed to other events. This is why many of us can't explain why we get headaches or why we have panic attacks or why we have nightmares or why we have problems sleeping. It's because we've suppressed (or think we've gotten over) the originating distressing and disturbing experiences. Some traumas start chain reactions of dysfunctional behaviors. Only after we commit to digging through our pasts and transparently facing every event that happened in our lives can we begin to pull the string of cause and effect that will uncover the cause of our dysfunctional behavior and live unfiltered, fulfilling lives. Let's take a look at how my string of dysfunctional behavior began to connect and grow, and then how I was able to unravel the messiness.

SMOKING MIRROR FREEDOM

I thought I had gotten away alive and well—away from the physical abuse, the alcoholism, and the family generational curse. Though I'd left home and thought I had outrun the family curse, I had no idea it was traveling within me.

Late one night in the dorm, I woke up drenched in a cold sweat, my pulse racing, my shirt sticking to me. If I rolled to my right, the sheets were soaked. If I rolled to my left, the sheets were soaked. I hadn't been having a nightmare. The AC was working. My roommate was fast asleep. What could it be? I felt both sides of my throat and face. I wasn't running a fever. Peeling the covers back and sitting up, I felt fine, not dizzy or lightheaded. What I did feel was anxiety. I felt like, deep down beneath my skin, my soul was jolting back and forth in convulsions. But I didn't know why. It wasn't exam season. I wasn't facing any disciplinary action. I racked my brain, trying to think of a just cause, but nothing came to mind. I thought maybe a nice walk in the cool night air would do me some good.

Even though it was around two o'clock in the morning, I got dressed in a pair of jeans and a T-shirt and went for it. Surprisingly, nobody was out on campus. All the dorms were dark and quiet. Passing the campus quad, I kept trying to figure out why I had woken up in such a flutter. I sat on the steps in front of the School of Business building. I hadn't realized how beautiful the front of campus was lit up at night. From the bricked driveway to the library to the auditorium, the floodlights bounced off the glass and twinkled.

Thirsty, I started walking the half-mile to the 7-Eleven. *Wow!*

I thought. *This little town doesn't sleep.* The highway was busy, and people were actually at the convenience store getting gas. Entering the store, I chose a Mountain Dew from the soda coolers and then headed to the register. There was a line. At two o'clock in the morning, there was a line? I couldn't believe it. I paid for my soda and starting walking back to campus. Only one car was getting gas.

As I walked past the gas pumps, someone suddenly grabbed my arm and started pulling me into the woods beside the store. I snatched my arm away but he grabbed me again. The stranger attempting to abduct me stood about five-ten, a full six inches taller than me. As I struggled to get away, I heard someone from the car at the gas pumps calmly say, "Her life or yours?" The abductor dropped my arm and ran.

The passenger from the car at the gas pump told me, "Get your ass in this damn car!" He looked familiar but I couldn't place his face. I couldn't remember where I'd seen him before or how I knew him, but somehow getting in the car felt safer than walking back to campus. The passenger asked if I'd gotten left by my ride, if other college students left me at the store and didn't come back to get me. After about seven rapid-fire questions, I could tell he was trying to figure out why I would be walking that late at night by myself. He fussed and cussed at me the whole ride back to campus so bad that the driver said, "Ease up, homie. She's got a right to walk to the store."

Before I got out, the passenger said, "And don't let me catch your little ass out here walking this late at night again." In class the next morning it hit me—I remembered. He was the boyfriend of one of the local girls that took classes at the college.

Though I did experience more episodes that woke me in the night, I either walked around campus or borrowed a car and drove around town. I never walked off campus at night again, but it would be years before I figured out why I had so casually put myself in danger that night without a second thought.

ON TOP OF THE WORLD

After graduating and earning my bachelor's, I attended graduate school and then lived in a few different states before settling in the Washington, DC, metro area. I'd bought my first home and felt absolutely on top of the world until—there it was again, two o'clock in the morning—this energy, this overwhelming feeling of fear and the choking sensation. I had no reason to feel that. I'd just moved into my brand-new home. Yay! I was gainfully employed. Heck, I'd just received an almost fifty-percent raise in salary (praise the good Lord!). My commute was ten minutes. I could wear jeans to work. I had food, clothing, transportation, good health, and shelter. I didn't need or want for anything. So why couldn't I catch my breath? Why couldn't I sleep? I knew what I needed—some peaceful night air. A nice stroll around the pond would help me sleep. And it did.

UNCOVERING THE SOURCE

Two o'clock in the morning. It was always around two o'clock in the morning. Waking up like I had just finished three four-hundred-meter dashes. Here I was again …

I ran through a laundry list of current events in my life but there was nothing to make me nervous. Nothing to intimidate me. But there it was again, the anxiety. The airplane turbulence way deep down in my soul. As always I got up, got dressed, and went for a walk out in the peaceful night air, but this time, I began to beseech God, over and over, "Lord, I pay my own mortgage. I live alone. Why am I out in the street walking in the middle of the night?"

Taking slow, deep breaths really calmed my system. I had walked less than a quarter of a mile when I felt a rush of calmness. All the nervous energy stopped flowing. The feeling of electricity rushing within me came to a halt. It was as if time had stopped and I was the only person that existed on the face of the planet. Instead of the feeling of electric shock, I felt a warm comforting glow of illumination.

God said, "It is over. Your peace is now in me," and it resonated over and over, not quite a repeating voice, but not quite an echo.

I replied, "Thanks, but you didn't answer my question. That's not what I asked you!" Seconds later, I had flashbacks so clear they played like holograms against the midnight sky. I watched myself being beaten in the middle of the night. I saw myself running into the cool night air as if it was a comforting, consoling parent cuddling a scared child. Suddenly, it all made sense.

The sweating, the shortness of breath, the sudden feeling of fear and choking—they were all flashbacks of traumatic events from my childhood. Experiences I had tucked away as though they were over and unrelated to my current life. However, my episodes in the night mimicked the time of the occurrences and the emotions of the events. The triggers were visits to my childhood home, my mother's house, but that revelation in 2005 was my last date with the cool night air.

LESSON TO LEARN

One of the ways childhood trauma creates adult dysfunctional behavior is through desensitization. I didn't see anything wrong with taking a walk at two o'clock in the morning because I had been exposed to it so often as a form of comfort and safety due to the abuse from my brother. The walks I took at night were a direct result of and imitated my running to the school at night to escape my brother's attacks. I had become oblivious to the dangers. Being out at night had become a refuge to me versus a hazard. This type of behavior is dysfunctional. Not simply because I was out at night, but because I was not conscious of the risk. The dysfunction had become normalized. Do you have any behaviors that are so ingrained you are no longer conscious of the danger? Where did it originate? Can you turn it around? Don't worry, the technique and activity below will help you discover your answers to these questions.

7-STEP
METHOD AFFIRMATION

I am the master of my emotions. I control them, they don't control me.

7-STEP METHOD TECHNIQUE
TRACK AND TRACE YOUR LIFE

In the previous chapter we created Life Maps that show us the terrain of our lives. We identified events that could be the "cause" of our untrue beliefs and dysfunctional behavior. In Step Two of my 7-Step Method, we will record the days of our lives as they happen, the "effects." The days of our lives are filled with our feelings and behaviors. The patterns of our feelings and behaviors are the links between our past and our present, our cause and effect, how we behave and why we behave the way we do. To get the full benefit of this step, you must go deeper than superficial small talk and write more about your feelings and beliefs. You must delve into how you felt and why you felt the way you did. What you believe is at the root of how you feel and behave. To help you get started, download my Trace Your Life Quick Starter at ThatAnitaLive.com/bk1. It's a list of questions to move you from the surface to a deeper level of journaling.

7-STEP METHOD ACTIVITY
TRACK AND TRACE YOUR LIFE

To do this, begin keeping a journal. Journaling will help you see the patterns in your life. Start each entry with the date and time. Then, along with your daily activities, the events you attend, tasks you complete, and people you interact with, be sure to include how each one made you feel—did it add something positive to your life or something negative? Don't edit, don't leave anything to memory, just write. Don't think first and decide what to write second, just write.

Once a quarter, go back and read your journal. While reading, identify the negative and positive. Highlight major decisions, habits/repetitive behavior, jokes, and emotions. Next, write in your journal the answers to these questions: How did that habit form? How long have you been practicing that habit? Why did you make each major decision? What did you believe that caused you to make that decision? And most importantly, what were the emotions that went along with the end result of the decision? Is it a decision you should change the next time you're faced with making it? Are your habits creating negative cycles? Are you existing or living?

COMING UP NEXT

I'll show you how my being exposed to abuse directly and indirectly created desensitization that led to my experiencing horrifying events like having an assault rifle pointed in my face, five days of my freedom taken away, cyclic public opinion of condemnation, and a decade of being ostracized and rejected.

Chapter Four

HOW TO ENFORCE YOUR BOUNDARIES

"For whoever does the will of My Father who is in heaven,
he is My brother and sister and mother."
Matthew 12:50 (NASB), Jesus Christ

BOUNDARIES

People in your life are either taking from you or giving to you. Very rarely do we get both from the same person. It's possible, but rare. Consider whether the people who take from you value what they take. Are they learning from it? Or are they taking from you to harm you, to dominate you and take advantage of you? In an interview with *Ebony* in November 1986, Tina Turner said, "If you are unhappy with anything—your mother, your father, your husband, your wife, your job, your boss, your car—whatever is bringing you down, get rid of it. You'll find that when you're free, your true creativity, your true self comes out." Who better to teach us about boundaries and knowing our worth than the legend herself?

You've heard the ole saying, you teach people how to treat you. Well, imagine living in a home where someone could verbally and physically attack you at any time and you had no recourse, no protection. It sifts away your self-defenses. When you've lived in the midst of one abusive situation after another, it desensitizes your reactions. It lowers your expectation for change. It's as if you've been in the same car accident so many times, those same ole wounds are numb and your tolerance for impact is high. Your boundaries have been pushed so far back, you don't teach people how to treat you because you've given up on anything ever being different. You feel as if nobody cares about you but you—so you just go with the flow until you can escape and move on.

So far we've examined the passive behavior of my mother, the aggressive behavior of my sibling, and the direct mental, emotional, and physical abuse I endured. Now, let's look at how becoming desensitized to dysfunctional behavior can make a person blind to the signs of future abuse.

TRUE STORY
HANDCUFFED AND TRAUMATIZED

Legion and I met online in the summer of 2005. As summer turned into fall, then winter, we moved from email to online chatting to phone calls. We met in person on vacation in Paris during the spring. Immediately, our personalities clicked. He liked all the same things I liked, including living in the moment and not looking for a relationship. We enjoyed visiting the Eiffel Tower and the Louvre and loved authentic French food.

When I returned to the States, we kept in touch. He asked me to accompany him on an Alaskan cruise that he was planning as a vacation during the summer. I agreed. However, during the cruise, things felt different. He wasn't the jovial, agreeable fellow I'd met in France. He was quiet. His comments and conversation were abrupt and rude. One defining moment happened on a sightseeing excursion away from the ship. He turned to me and calmly said, "I could kidnap you and no one would know. I could hold you in an abandoned building and torture you until you die." Inside, I froze. Outside, I kept a cool demeanor and walked back to the ship as quickly as possible.

After I returned home from the cruise, I started distancing myself slowly. I'd seen enough fatal relationships to know you don't make sudden moves on unstable men. I made it clear our friendship was over and I asked him not to call me anymore, but the more I didn't answer, the more he called. Day after day, my phone would ring back to back. He would hang up and dial again instead of letting the voicemail pickup.

FRIDAY, SEPTEMBER 1, 2006

Again my desk phone and my cell phone rang off the hook all day with his phone number showing in the caller ID—but no message. I didn't answer. Driving home from work, I turned off the ringer on my cell phone and stuck it in my purse. The constant ringing from him calling back to back day and night for weeks on end had become nerve-racking.

At home I tried to have a conversation with a friend on the phone, but he kept beeping in. Unable to have a conversation, I hung up with my friend and answered his call.

"What do you want now?" I answered.

"You didn't go to work today?"

I didn't answer the question. He was trying to bait me into an argument so that in defense of myself, I would give him information he didn't have.

"Why is that your business?" I asked. "This is over. We are no longer friends. Why are you calling me? Leave me alone!"

"I'm just calling to check on you. I know how hard breakups can be."

"Breakups? Who do you think you're fooling? I have your phone number. If I wanted to talk to you, I'd call you, but I didn't—"

"We can't just have a conversation?" he interrupted.

"No!"

"Well, did you go get the gun I told you to get?"

"Gun? I told you, that is your world, not mine."

"DC is a very dangerous place. You need to be able to protect yourself."

The only person I need protection from is you. I thought it, but I didn't say it. "If I tell you I got it, will you leave me alone? I can't even talk on my phone for you beeping in and interrupting my phone calls. You've got other people you can see. Go live your life!"

On the cruise, he'd asked me if I owned a gun and tried to convince me to purchase one. While the DC, Maryland, and Virginia area has had its fair share of crime, I did not have a gun and had no intention of purchasing one. I'd lived among crime and faced abuse my entire life and survived well without one. I'd always felt the ole urban saying was true, "When you live by the gun, you die by the gun," meaning when you bring a gun into your life, karma brings everything that comes with it, good and bad.

He continued, "Well, I don't think you should kill yourself."

Sarcastically I responded, "What? Well, thank you. Enjoy your evening." And I hung up.

I was lost as to how to get away from him; honesty, sarcasm, and Tactical Ignoring were not working. Considering the sharpshooter training he'd told me he had, the wars he'd served in, the area of swing in his personality pendulum, and his inability to let go, I grew concerned for my safety. Creating a safety plan is paramount, so let me repeat: you can't make sudden moves on unstable men. Ladies, please remember this. Too many of us die at the hands of men we know from making unplanned sudden moves, but back to my story. I've had friends go to prison for murder and I've had friends that were murdered. I kept thinking about those four women at Fort Bragg all murdered within six weeks' time by members of the military. It scared me, but the victim never has a voice. She's never taken seriously until after she's dead. Who could I turn to?

It started again. Five times my cell phone rang before there was a brief pause, then five more rings. Again and again, he called.

I answered, "Would you please leave me alone!"

"I don't want you to kill yourself."

"I don't know where you're getting that from—"

He interrupted, yelling at the top of his voice, asking me if I knew anyone that had committed suicide. He named a litany of different people from cousins, aunts, and uncles to schoolmates to coworkers, finding it impossible that I didn't know anyone who had ever committed suicide. I didn't. I simply replied no and tried to stay as quiet as possible to calm him down until I could get off the phone.

Next he asked, "If you tried to commit suicide, how would you do it?"

His voice seem to deescalate a little.

"I never would commit suicide," I told him.

Returning to yelling again, he asked, "Well, just suppose, if you did, how would you do it?"

"I wouldn't do it. My life is not my own."

"Your life is your own. Nobody owns you!" He was yelling at the top of his lungs. "Now, tell me, if you were to try to kill yourself, how would you do it?"

"I don't know what you're dealing with, but if someone wants to take their own life, there is nothing you can do about it."

"Well, suppose you took a lot of pills?" He was still yelling.

"That depends on the amount of active ingredients that were in the pills and how my system reacted. It doesn't mean I would automatically die. I could survive as a vegetable. Which ain't pretty."

"Ok, you don't take pills. You block the exhaust and lock yourself in your car?"

He told me this was how his father died, which I thought would cause him to become more agitated, but he began to calm down. I wondered if he was having flashbacks between war time and childhood abuse. He continued to name a number of different ways a person could take their own life. I simply agreed with whatever he said, praying that someone else would very soon become his object of attention.

I continued to answer, "Then I guess I would suffocate and die. Isn't that the objective?"

"Well, what if you weren't in your car but in your house? You'd make a mess."

"I'd do what?" The spin lost me but I was too scared to agitate him more, so I just listened and agreed.

Legion's anger seemed to subside. I felt like this was my chance to get off the line, but before I could end the call, the fax machine in the kitchen started to ring over and over. I got out of bed, walked downstairs, and unplugged it.

He asked, "Is that your home phone ringing?"

"Yes."

"That's the police. They want to talk to you."

"What? About what? And why would they call you? How do you know who it is?"

"They want to talk to you!"

I clicked over to find it was in fact the police. Sgt. Steed asked, "What's going on in there?"

I was dumbfounded and in shock. All I could think was, why are *you* calling *me* out of the blue about what is going on in the privacy of *my own* home? The question was odd, but I told the truth, I said, "Nothing." She asked if she could come in, but before I could answer, she asked if I would come outside. I said, "Sure, let me get a jacket." I got my rain jacket and went out through my garage where I was met by a man dressed in all black who was pointing an assault rifle in my face.

At the top of the hill, I saw five police cars and about twenty police officers blocking off my dead-end street, which was only 150ft and had just twelve houses on it. Two officers stayed outside with me while the rest went into my home. I asked one of the officers outside why they were in my house. He told me they were looking for the gun. I asked, "What gun?" I later found out they had evacuated all of my neighbors and blocked off my entire neighborhood to thru traffic.

He said, "The caller said you had a gun."

I asked, "What caller? And you just believe some random caller?" The officer shrugged his shoulders, turned, and resumed his football conversation with his coworker. There we stood in the rain.

About an hour later, all the officers came rushing out of the house and formed a very tight circle around me. It was highly uncomfortable to have strange men that close to my body. I got really frightened and shaken. I was terrified that they were about to beat me within inches of my life like so many others. I thought, *Oh my God, this is it, I am going to die.* They asked me for the gun and my keys. I told them I didn't have a gun, and I didn't know where my keys were. *How did they expect a woman to think, being physically threatened by men twice her size with assault guns?* I reiterated that I didn't have a gun and asked why they needed my keys.

Sgt. Steed responded, "Because you have to go to the precinct." I asked how long I would be gone. She responded, "Twenty minutes or so. You won't be down there long." (I found out later that was all a lie, and I never should have trusted the police.) So, I volunteered for the police to lock my house, and I would reenter via the garage code because I didn't know where my keys were. Five days later, a long way off from twenty minutes, I would return to find my home had been left wide open. None of the doors were locked. All my window treatments and blinds were wide open and all the lights had been turned on. The exact opposite of how I kept my home. Passers-by could see straight through my home and see everything in it, including the fact that no one was there.

I arrived at the precinct a little after seven in the evening. The lights were out, so I sat in the dark for hours with one other officer. I had no idea why I was there, why they'd searched my home. If I was being charged with anything, I was absolutely clueless. I didn't even have my purse, ID, or any money. All I had were my cell phones.

A little after one o'clock in the morning, a lady came over and started asking me questions. She didn't introduce herself or say who she was or why she was asking me so many questions. She wasn't in a police uniform. She asked me my name, address, and what reason did I have to live. I gave her my name and address but repeated the last question in disbelief, "What reason do I have to live?" *Who says I get to make that decision?* I told her I live because He lives, because God lives. She rolled her eyes, sighed, and stomped out of the room. When she returned, she asked if I had any pets. I told her no. She asked why I'd told the caller I was going to kill myself. By then I had figured out that the caller was Legion. I said I never told him that. She rolled her eyes and said she was going to talk to him. I asked if she was going to talk to any of my other friends. She screamed, "No!" and left the room! About thirty-minutes later, she reentered the room for a third time.

This time she exclaimed, "He says you did say it!"

"He's lying."

"He says you're mad because he broke it off with you."

"Ma'am, I am the one trying to end it, and it's simple—all he has to do is stop calling me. I have nothing that belongs to him. We don't share friends, enemies, or children. My friends don't even know he exists. I haven't answered one of his calls all day. I only answered his call this evening because I couldn't have a conversation with anyone else because of his constant beeping in."

She yelled, "You don't know! I can keep you! There'll have to be a court hearing and everything!"

I asked, "Keep me? Why would you keep me?"

She left the room and slammed the door, and my heart started to race. I paced the room. I thought about the twenty minutes Sgt. Steed told me this would take. It had been eight hours.

There were two things I couldn't understand and one thing I noticed about the lady that kept entering and exiting the room: One, why was she so angry? Two, why was she so angry at me? And three, why did she smell of alcohol? I later learned she was from the Virginia Community Services Board and was responsible for assessing whether or not I was a threat to myself and others. Yet she only asked me to confirm his story. She didn't question me for truth or ask me any open-ended questions. Her only questions were intended to prove his version of the story. What kind of assessment is that?

About two hours later, an officer handcuffed me, and two of them drove me to the county hospital emergency room. During the drive, they talked to each other, one officer telling the other, "This is babysitting. We shouldn't have to do this. We only have to stay here forty-five minutes. After that, whether they have taken her or not, we can leave and if she walks out of here, it's not our problem."

While we were waiting to be checked in, I asked the officer if I could see the paperwork. He replied sure and handed it to me. Turns out, Legion had called the police in my county from halfway across the world and told them I was trying to shoot myself because he wouldn't marry me. My mind raced trying to figure out why he thought I even wanted to be married at all. I hadn't mentioned marriage. I wasn't buying wedding magazines. I hadn't asked him to marry me. We had just met in person a few months ago, and you only begin to get to know someone when you meet them in person. I couldn't think of anything. The desk clerk called the officer over.

Checking me in, the desk clerk asked for my name, address, and Social Security number. They ran blood and urine tests—all clean! The doctor asked me what happened. I told him the police called me to come outside, searched my home, took me to the precinct, and now I was there.

He said he would see if he could get me released, but he returned with bad news. The magistrate had signed an order, making detainment mandatory. Apparently, if you've been in custody over four hours and will not volunteer to be detained, the magistrate signs to detain you by force.

I was walked to another room and handed off to a nurse, who asked for my clothes. Shocked, I looked at her and asked for clarity, "My clothes?" Her eyes filled with water as she stared at the floor. She couldn't even look at me as she said, "I don't know what happened." Her voice cracked. "Your case just doesn't make any sense to any of us, and is not the type we usually see here, but I'm sorry..." She almost started crying. She handed me a set of scrubs and a brown bag for my belongings, and closed the door behind her as she left. I could tell she knew I didn't belong there, especially after she left me alone to change my clothes. People on suicide watch are never left alone, especially if their personal belongings have not been confiscated.

I was assigned to a room and given a quart-sized plastic bag containing deodorant, soap, toothpaste, and a comb. The comb I couldn't use; the spaces between the teeth were too small (a sister was ten weeks out from a touch-up and had just stood in the rain for over an hour). The nurse then walked me to a caseworker who completed some paperwork and escorted me to an assigned room.

Fifteen minutes later, another caseworker entered, introduced herself, and asked what I was thinking about. I told her I was trying to figure out what I had done to cause this. She asked me what had happened. I told her. She gave me an overview of the daily itinerary. I told her I would just stay in my room to try to get through this. She told me not to do that because then they would think something was wrong even if it wasn't. And being a holiday weekend, my case wouldn't be heard until Tuesday, a four day wait.

In hindsight it made sense—to most people isolation is a sign of depression but, being an introvert, it reenergizes me and gives me time to connect to my Creator and recharge. To forego being misunderstood, I had to suppress my real feelings and put my game face on. Looking back, I appreciate her honesty. It was obvious she also knew I didn't belong there.

Off to breakfast I went.

SATURDAY, SEPTEMBER 2, 2006

I moved the food around on the tray so that it would look like I'd eaten, but I couldn't bear the tastelessness of the food. As the new girl, I entertained my fellow detainees' questions and was surprised to learn many people sign themselves in to dry out over the weekend or to escape the dysfunction in their homes.

After breakfast it was time to see the doctor—a psychiatrist, I presumed. He asked me what had happened. I told him. He asked if I wanted any Thorazine. I said no. End of appointment. I was in his office less than five minutes. Though he was talking to me, he was preoccupied with his phone. He never looked up at me. I'm not sure if it was a tactic or technique, but the eyes are the window to the soul. If he wanted to accurately assess me, the least he had to do was look at me.

Later in the day, the case worker returned and asked how I was doing. I said I was participating but couldn't wait to regain my freedom so that I could begin to process and heal from the ordeal.

As time passed, I got to know some detainees better than others. One of the patients was an elderly African American lady. I'm not sure why, but she followed me around. Wherever I sat, she sat; wherever I went, she went. She would smile at me as if she could see something in me no one else could. Two others, a thin Caucasian dude and a young African American guy, took to me and sat wherever I sat.

During workshop time, the Caucasian guy asked what I was doing in there. He said it was kind of obvious I didn't belong—maybe it was all my correct answers to the workshop questions. I kind of felt bad. I wanted to continue to put my best foot forward so that I could be freed, but part of me wondered if I shouldn't sink back and be reserved so that the others could get the attention they signed themselves into the hospital to get.

Later in the day I was sitting in the front area with some of the other detainees, and one of them was banging her head against the wall. The doctor yelled at her, "Stop it! Stop it! What—you want me to lose my job?" His yelling caught the attention of the two detainees sitting with me; I had been watching it unfold since they entered the area. Chitchatting with other detainees, I said, "He's no shrink and she ain't crazy."

The white guy I talked to during the workshop said, "Yes, she is, 'Nita. She's in here all the time. She signs herself in when she feels episodes coming on."

I said, "Whenever something happens she doesn't want to deal with, she checks herself in." I glanced at her again and continued, "Look. Pay attention to how she's banging her head—carefully, so she doesn't hurt herself. Crazy people feel no pain banging their heads because they are already drowning in it."

The white guy asked, "Well, what should the doctor do?"

"The doctor has a network of other doctors he can consult with to find out what works," I told him, "and he has a manual full of criteria, treatments, and exercises to try to help her. He isn't trying anything. It's like a surgeon standing over a broken leg, yelling at it to heal."

SUNDAY, SEPTEMBER 3, 2006

After breakfast we were sitting around the front area near the cafeteria. I looked down and saw keloids on the African American dude's wrists and asked what happened. He told me his girlfriend had decided she wanted to move on to another guy; he'd lost his will to live, so he'd started cutting his wrist.

I was shocked. Numb. I couldn't believe I was actually sitting with someone that didn't value himself more than anything or anyone else, someone that didn't love himself first. In my positions as a counselor I'd had clients threaten suicide, but sitting in a chair yelling and crying is very different from doing. I've also had dear friends call me with suicidal thoughts, but none of them ever had a complete plan of action.

I told him, "Look … see that red book on the desk in the fish bowl?" I was referring to the office where all the county workers sat; it was half-glass, floor to ceiling, and reminded me of a fish bowl. Pointing through the case workers' window at the book, I said, "That book is called the DSM-IV, *The Diagnostic and Statistical Manual of Mental Disorders, Version Four*. In that book is every emotional and mental problem a person could have, the symptoms of each one, and how to treat it. If your doctor has not given you a diagnosis that's in that book, your problem is an affair of the heart, not your head. Either way, I want you to do me a favor. Around the corner is a church called First AME."

He said, "I know it. My cousin goes to that church."

"Ok, good," I said. "You know exactly how to find it then. But you aren't going for church—you're going for Jesus. Every Sunday, go to that church, sit in the back, and listen to the sermon. Don't worry about a ministry. When people come over to you and try to get you to attend other things, smile and tell them you just need the Word right now. You can even get there late and leave early. Concentrate on the Word. Monday through Saturday, read your Bible. Even if you only read a verse a day. Read your Bible. Whenever those thoughts of harming yourself or killing yourself come to mind, find you a good Bible verse that feels right and repeat it constantly—"

"I tried repeating stuff to myself," he interrupted me. "It didn't work."

"This ain't stuff," I continued. "This is the Word of God, and if you ask—if you call—He will answer. If it seems like repeating the Word to yourself isn't helping, then go all out into full conversation with Jesus and get busy doing something—playing solitaire, listening to gospel music, building a house out of cards, dancing, something. And in conversation with God, tell Him—"

"*Tell* God?" he interrupted.

"Yes! Tell!" I said. "Challenge Him based on the Word you have learned. Say to Him, 'God, you promised that if I called, you would answer. I'm fighting and need your help. The devil is after me, and he's winning and I'm losing. Help!' Say it. Say it out loud. Say it until you fall asleep, notice time has slipped away, or realize it has stopped. I guarantee you if you call Him, *He will answer.*"

The evening case worker came by and suggested I call family to go to my house and bring me my allergy prescription. *Who do they think I would let in my house when I'm not home? Why would they take for granted I had family in the area, as transient as the Washington DC area is? Why would they take either of those for granted?* I said, "Ma'am, I don't have any family in the area."

"Well, I'm just doing what they told me to do," she replied.

That afternoon, the case worker came to my room when I returned from the doctor and asked if I had called any relatives. I told her I didn't have any. She said it would look better at the hearing if I had some family there with me. I told her I wasn't from the area and didn't have anybody, though I was thinking that even if my bio-fam were here in the area, I wouldn't call them. The last thing I needed during the toughest time in my life was to be around people who speak fear, doubt, death, and condemnation. The last thing I needed to hear was, "Look at what you done got yourself into now. I told you—you need a man! I told you, you need to come home! You think you can survive here by yourself! You think you can take care of yourself!"

No, thank you. I'll take my chances with Jesus. Just me and Jesus.

When I got called in to see the doctor again, he told me he was recommending that they keep me another week because he didn't believe my story. I asked what investigation would be done. He said they didn't do investigations.

I asked, "So how am I being evaluated? What is my DSM-IV diagnosis?" He shrugged his shoulders, so I asked, "On what basis are you keeping me?"

"It's my recommendation. I'm the doctor," he told me, again never even looking at me during the whole conversation.

With every step back to my room, things became darker and darker. I'd lose my job. Lose my home and my right to vote, all because I had befriended the wrong human being. I imagined the sheriff throwing my treasured belongings out onto the street for trash pickup. My soft, supple, hand-dyed, aged leather loveseat. My Queen Anne chairs. My textbooks from grad school. My yearbooks and personal papers. Years of struggle and sacrifice to accomplish advanced education and to build a life for myself, reduced to worthless because one man was revengeful.

I went into the bathroom. Locking the door, I felt all my strength draining from my body. I dropped to the floor with my face between my knees, my soul crying out, "Jesus, I need you right now. I have no one else to call. Help!" The tears slowly streamed from my eyes and down my cheeks and dropped from my chin to the floor. I was broken. I didn't have the strength to stretch my arms or push my legs out from under me. The air I breathed out left my body but none returned.

Then I heard an illuminating voice whisper, "Get up before they miss you." I splashed my face with cold water and returned to the group.

TUESDAY, SEPTEMBER 5, 2006

Labor Day came and went, then finally it was Tuesday, the next business day. The hearings started at 9:00 a.m., and I was assigned the 10:30 a.m. slot. It wasn't much of a hearing. One man in an office. No plaintiff. No defense. I couldn't figure out why they hadn't subpoenaed the caller there to answer for making a false report. People can knowingly make false accusations about you and walk away without any effect on their life or punishment for lying. The police assume it's true, react instead of investigating, and your life is ruined. Nobody cares about you but you. There in that office on that Tuesday morning, I accepted that.

Even though the doctor had recommended I continue to be detained, he wasn't even there, and the administrator facilitating the hearing decided to let me go. I was told I had to meet with a counselor to set up follow-up appointments after release, and the counselor was waiting in the hallway right outside the door. She told me I had a choice between two offices. I asked who the counselor would be because I couldn't see the lady that had detained me in the first place based on an accusation—a false report—from one person halfway around the world and no evidence. She decided to take the case herself. When I did see her for a follow-up session weeks later, the first question she asked me was how I knew so much about counseling and psychology. She was the first person to ask a question about me and not try to simply prove the caller right. For that I was thankful. Unfortunately, the question was based on an age-old prejudice that says, unless a black woman is grinning ear to ear like she has two pebbles for brains, she's presumed mentally ill because (they think) there is no way she could be intelligent. Ugh! It's unfortunate she had to ask, but I'm glad she did.

I changed into my own clothes, collected my belongings, which had been placed in a brown bag, and exited the building. Turning my phone on, I had seventeen messages from Legion, already recanting his story.

I got home and struggled to maintain the routine I had before the incident. My phone rang continuously back to back, so I turned it off. The next morning, I got up and went to work. All day my thoughts fluctuated between revenge and keeping myself safe. Various forms of vindication vividly played out in my mind: Food poisoning. Worn brake-fluid lines on his vehicle. House fire. Dismemberment. My desk phone rang two to three times an hour with his phone number showing on the caller ID. I still hadn't turned my cell phone back on.

That evening after I got home, I checked my voicemail messages. He'd left me a message that said if I didn't call him back, he would be in my house when I got home the next day. *Damn, now what do I do? I can't even dial 911 because they've already taken his side and believed him without any consideration of me or my life.*

Wednesday, the next day at work, the switchboard operator for the building called. She said she had an emergency phone call for me and asked if I wanted her to patch it through. I heard two tones then silence.

I said, "Hello?"

He started screaming at the top of his lungs. "You can't even be appreciative of someone that is trying to show concern for you! I'm just trying to help you out! Do I need to call them again? You know they'll believe me over you, don't you? I'll do it!"

Tears streamed down my face. *My God, how do I get out of this?* I didn't say a word. He went on explaining that he would do it again if I didn't visit him the coming weekend. I put the receiver down on the desk and closed the door to my office.

When I picked up the phone, he was still screaming, "See what I can do to you? See what I can do to you?"

After about a month, his friends started to call on his behalf, asking me to talk to him and to see him. I continued to spend time with Legion only because I feared for my safety. I was completely lost about what to do. I thought my only hope was to wait until someone else demanded his time and he decided to leave. Every ninety days or so, he would spaz out, threaten to call the cops again, then stop calling for about twenty-four to forty-eight hours before calling again and acting as if nothing had happened or somehow it was all my fault. I felt numb and hopeless.

A VOICE OF REASON

I took my confusion to a colleague. We knew each other well from both social and professional circles. He and I had just started working for the same company. I planned to give him the thirty-minute version of the characters in play, the tumultuous events, and the pendulum swings.

About fifteen minutes in, he said, "Wait ... question. How come you never brought him around us or to any of our events? Hold on, I thought you were dating somebody else."

"Because part-timers don't get full-timers' benefits." His chin dropped, leaving his mouth wide open. I continued to give details, then wrapped up the quick version by asking, "Now, how do I get out of this and live?"

My colleague of six years leaned forward and slowly and very intently said, "Nita, these people need lives of their own. You are not abnormal. They have just never been exposed to anything unlike them. All you have to do is walk away, and we both know you know how to do that."

I thought about what he'd said for days. It made perfect sense. In hindsight, I had been so wrapped up in the spin and swirl of fear and confusion that I just couldn't see my way clear. I stopped answering my phone and that was that. Though I was highly anxious and nervous for a period of time, I did get to move on with my life.

I did receive blocked ID calls for years after. I also received calls from odd telephone numbers. Whenever I researched those numbers in Intelius.com or USSearch.com, the report always listed the name of one of his relatives, but for all intents and purposes, I was free.

LESSON TO LEARN

Did you see the connections between childhood trauma and adult dysfunction? I was way too passive in handling this situation. Because I had become so used to enduring emotional abuse, I thought I could shield myself from any harm because I knew what he was saying wasn't true. I thought that if I slowly distanced myself, I could get away—alive.

In my past, whenever I ignored someone they went away. Not Legion. The less I answered the phone, the more he called. When I refused to visit him, he called the police, and I felt trapped. I felt like my only choices were death or abuse. Because his abuse was verbal and not physical, it was my word against his. My childhood was replaying. I was left to solve this life-threatening situation on my own. So I did the only thing I knew how—endure it in silence until something gave me an out. Because I was alone.

This is what many of you go through every day, suffering in silence, making a dysfunctional existence in this world normal. Experiencing life in a state of numbness and repetitive prayer that someone will save you without any effort on your part, but that is not going to happen. You have to make the commitment to change your life, to stop going in circles. Start your journey to emotional healing today. Yes, it is a journey, there are no quick fixes. You must be dedicated to the pursuit of living free from emotional baggage. You will be tried and tested for the rest of your life. Every time you feel you have overcome, circumstances will throw another bag of trash at you in the form of a test. But you can win. Make the choice to fight for healthy. I did. And I've never looked back.

MOVING ON

After the Labor Day ordeal, I had to let a lot of people go. I had to cut them clean and completely out of my life with no explanation. People I thought knew me better, people that had heard about the incident through the grapevine but never asked me about it or brought it up for conversation. They never showed sincere concern, yet their behavior toward me changed. I cut them off because everyone is free to believe what they want, but they are not free to treat me as if what they believe is true.

LETTING GO OF THEM
TO LOVE YOU

Every person is supposed to have a safe place to exist: a supportive family, loving friends, a cove-like place that encourages their soul, nourishes their spirit, and provides lift to their wings so they can soar in life.

But what do you do if you're not born into such a situation? You create it. Could you let go of any person, place, or thing that weighs you down, causes you harm, or creates barriers to your growth and maturity? Your mom? Your church? Your adult child? Your job? Your spouse?

It was time. As I looked back over the last few years of my life, I'd been praying to be set free—not just free from my bio-family, but free from the world. I'd done everything in life I had set out to do. I prayed, "God, I'm done. My bucket list is completely punched, so if all you have for my life is what I'm doing now—working and paying bills—this is a wrap. Swing the pearly gates open, give Apostle Peter the keys to the best chariot, and tell him to swing low. Tell Tupac to meet me out front, and have Frank 'Ole Blue Eyes' Sinatra and Sammy Davis Jr. serenade me as this saint comes marching into heaven. Go!"

I was done with Earth, but God wasn't done with me. Through a series of events, he let me know that under no circumstances were the apostles, the archangels, or the Holy Mother Mary to have pity on me and beseech him on my behalf for such a ridiculous request.

So I went in—inside me. I sought to learn more about me, my existence, and the purpose for it. When you take the time to connect with your innermost self, in those moments you will find your truth, your peace, and your purpose. You will discover the courage you need to be alone. The bravery you need to set boundaries and allow intimate access to only those people who show you they value you, respect you, build you up, and add meaning to your life.

THE PROCESS OF LETTING GO

After that incident, I had to let go of a lot of so-called friends. But the process of letting go of family had been developing in my life for years. In 1989 I began to decrease the number of return visits to my childhood home. I only returned for weddings, funerals, and family reunions. I thought if I decreased the number of visits, it would decrease the occurrence of new abusive incidents. I was wrong. While one needs to be present for physical abuse to occur, this is not true for mental and emotional abuse. In 1993 I discontinued any communication with my sibling. In 1996 I stopped giving family members my physical address and opted to only share my post office box. In 2000 I stopped giving my mother my work phone number after her second attempt at trying to have me fired from my job. Still, at any time, I could answer my phone and my mother would be fussing, screaming, and shouting on the other end, so in 2001 I activated a second cell phone so I could separate my bio-family from my regular life. This helped me maintain calmness and peace because I only answered the fam-phone if I was at home and could take the time to recenter myself emotionally after the call. However, each phone call, wedding, funeral, or any other event that mandated a visit to my childhood home resulted in a fresh wound.

After decades of waking up with fists pounding into my flesh, being choked until I passed out, being told nobody wanted to be bothered with me, being consistently told I wasn't smart enough, after years of dealing with my father being a homicidal alcoholic and my mother being neglectful, it was time for a decision.

THE FINAL FAMILY STRAW

One of the last abusive events I experienced happened in 2013, the last time I was with my bio-fam. I allowed my mother to talk me into attending a family event, and we were all staying at her house—my brother, his wife and children, our mom, and me in a three-bedroom, one-bathroom house. I tried to spend most of my time in my bedroom with the door closed, but this visit seemed to be calm and quiet. It was almost eerie.

The day before I was to leave, I had just gotten out of the bathtub and returned to my bedroom to dry off and get dressed when the door opened. My brother stood their gawking at my naked body. I felt violated. Humiliated. Ashamed. I grabbed the door, but he held it open. I had to push with all my bodyweight to get the door shut. But right there in my humiliated nakedness I made the decision this would be the last time. It became very clear the reason they continued to abuse me was because I kept giving them access. I left my mother's home at seventeen, her purse at twenty-five, and have never had to return to either. I had no reason to keep returning to this house or these people.

I got dressed and ran through the hallway, the dining room, the living room, off the porch, down the sidewalk, and into the street—the same pathway I'd run so many nights when I was younger to stop him from beating me. I ran up the hill and realized the one neighbor I used to run to for consolation had died, so I just continued to walk the town until night fell. I returned to the house, packed my belongings, and left.

Weeks later when I called back and told my mother what happened, she screamed, "That never happened!" and hung up the phone. The very next morning she called me like we'd never had that conversation. "Morning, sleepyhead," she sang. But I couldn't do it again. I couldn't pretend nothing had happened—again. When my father tried to set the house on fire, we both returned to our regularly scheduled activities like nothing had happened. When my brother was beating on me night after night and I cried out to her—nothing happened.

I explained to her that I would not live in the world of pretend and deny with her any longer. I told her when she was ready to acknowledge that her son's behavior was wrong and was ready to discuss that—call me. And I hung up. She called back and left a voicemail, asking what behavior and why didn't I tell her?

A year or so passed of more pretend-and-deny behavior, and then I made the final decision. I wrote her a letter explaining that she was free to live in Disney, but she could not force me to continue to reside there with her. A week or so later I followed up with a card, explaining that my phone would be disconnected and she would not receive the new phone number. I walked away. I got off the physically and emotionally abusive merry-go-round I'd been riding for forty years. I completely cut my family off and walked away.

FAMILY IS NOT EVERYTHING

As Bishop T.D. Jakes says, "It doesn't matter where you start, it matters where you finish." Or as Katie Perry said during the 2016 Democratic National Convention, "It doesn't matter where you start, but what you grow into."

Through all the seasons of my accomplishments, my bio-fam has been there berating me for my every move. Telling me I was inept and would surely fail. The long-handled spoon had been growing for a while; it just became time to break it.

The decision to cut off my family was not an easy one, nor did I take it lightly. However, as I had taken steps toward cutting my family off, the improvement in my life could not be denied. When I cut my siblings out of my life and put myself first, I went from being a C student to an A student. My family told me I wasn't smart enough to get an advanced degree—I earned two. They told me I didn't know how to move from one city to another—I've moved more than five times, not just city to city but state to state. They told me I couldn't buy a house—I've bought two. Clearly, family is not everything. How did I do it?

By using the affirmations, techniques, and activities of my 7-Step Method, along with the faith that Psalm 27:10 was absolutely true—that even when my mother and father forsake me, the Lord would hold me close.

Get this in your head, get this down in your spirit, hold this in your heart: it doesn't matter what you have endured, it doesn't matter how old you are, it doesn't matter what you've done in your life or what other people think of you—you are wonderfully made. You are a special treasure of the most-high all-powerful God, and He did not create you to allow people to use your imperfections as their ammunition to keep you bound, to keep you at a place in your life that is comfortable for them. Know that when you're down to zero and feel like you've got nothing, God is at the one, waiting for you to get up and rise again! You are heard! You are loved! You are powerful!

LESSON TO LEARN

Never give access to the wrong ones, not even family. Being silent, not expressing my displeasure about offenses, and being desensitized to danger put me in the perfect position to be preyed upon by other abusers. I was silent because of my exposure to domestic violence. I was withdrawn from true connection because of parental neglect, and I was desensitized to danger due to sibling abuse. Every incident of trauma pushes your emotional boundaries back more because it increases your desensitization to being mistreated. Again, childhood trauma creates adult dysfunctional behavior. Don't add insult to injury if you have been abused or even exposed to abuse. Take the time and complete the exercises to become more self-aware. Learn what your limiting beliefs and their root causes are, then put in the work to dispel them. There is a state of peace and an unspeakable joy on the other side of living emotionally unhealthy. Fight for healthy.

7-STEP
METHOD AFFIRMATION

Having boundaries shows I want self-respect.
Forcing people to adhere to my boundaries shows I have self-respect.

It's easy to tell people you will not tolerate their behavior anymore. It's also easy for them to listen, but when they repeat that same behavior over and over to your detriment, who will you choose—them or you? To experience emotional baggage breakthroughs, the negative behavior stops and gets dropped immediately—yours and theirs. In order to receive respect, you must first show respect for yourself.

7-STEP METHOD TECHNIQUE
DISPOSE OF DISTRACTIONS

Trying to mature in the midst of the same ole life is like trying to live in the eye of a tornado. It's impossible. Everything around you—what you watch, listen to, and say—affects you internally. The content you take in determines the creativity you give out. It affects your mood, thoughts, and feelings. Stop any behaviors that don't serve your new life: negative news broadcasts, toxic family, tormenting friends, emotional eating, retail therapy, adverse television shows, etc. Take a step back from your entertainment and consider the lyrics in the music you listen to. Take an objective look at the reality show you love to watch. If it is not a representation of the happier life you desire, it's stopping you from moving toward it.

7-STEP METHOD ACTIVITY
DISPOSE OF DISTRACTIONS

This activity is about lists. Download the "Dispose of Distractions Time Worksheet" from my website (ThatAnitalive.com/bk1) or make a list of timeslots in half-hour increments from the time you get up to the time you go to bed each day. Make thirty copies of the worksheet. Write a date for each day across the top, one date per sheet. Each day, every half hour, write the name of the person(s) you're with at that time—your spouse, office mates, quad-cube mates, commuter train rider, lunch mate, yoga instructor, karate parents, EVERYBODY! If you happen to be alone at the time, write your name. Next to each name, write an emotion describing how the interaction made you feel. Here are a few to get your emotion word bank started: scared, angry, happy, sad, ashamed, envious, anxious, demeaned, honored, supported, belittled, annoyed, optimistic, trusted, serene, and peaceful.

On Day 31, let's see who's in your Fab Five. First, go through your worksheets and make a separate list of all the names. Count the number of times each name appears on your sheets. Look at the numbers and determine which five people you spend the most time around.

Renowned businessman and speaker Jim Rohn says, "You're the average of the five people you spend most of your time around." Who are your most influential five? Do you want to become the average of those people? If not, how will you work to change that? Second, go through your "Dispose of Distraction Time Worksheets" and highlight all the negative emotions. Then make a list of each negative

111

emotion and the name associated with that negative emotion. Are you going to keep these people in your life? How will you change their effect on your emotions?

Before I close, I want to make one thing clear. I'm not telling you to do what I did. I'm simply showing you pieces of my life as examples of negative situations and the techniques I used to break through the dysfunction and harness my greatness for a better life. Do not feel you have to completely cut people out of your life like I did. TV and social media noise—yes. But people—no. Disposing of people—that's my issue. But I'll tell you what—nobody says it better than the famed family matriarch herself, Madea.

Tyler Perry's legendary character Mabel "Madea" Simmons teaches in the 2006 stage play *Madea Goes to Jail*:

"Some people come into your life for a lifetime, some come for a season. You got to know which is which. And you're going to always mess up when you mix them seasonal people up with lifetime expectations."

Here's how Madea tells us to decide who to let go and who to keep:

"Ain't nobody said it was gonna be easy, but it will get easy when you learn how to love yourself. When you get to a point in your life where you look at people and you go, 'Okay wait a minute. You or me?' you will make a decision. When you telling folks to do something … Now I've never thrown nobody away, I've never in my life just thrown anybody away saying, 'Don't bother me no more, don't talk to me no more,' I've never done that. What I do is tell them, 'Look, this thing you doing right here is gonna cause a problem. You need to fix that because if we're gonna be friends and we gonna be cool, you need to fix that. And if you don't, we're gonna have an issue.' If you see somebody fix it or even trying to fix it, that's somebody that cares, keep those people around, that's a leaf that's trying to grow up and be something else. But if you

tell somebody 'What you're doing is hurting me and I need you to stop' and they keep doing it, they don't care. Move on, let them go! No matter how much it hurts, let them go. It'll get easier, I promise you. Every day, it'll get easier and easier and easier, you just have to make it through."

Trust me—it hurt to let my mother go, but I had to choose … her or me. And for those of you that still feel I was wrong for walking away from my family—when Jesus lets Satan back into heaven, call me!

COMING UP NEXT

Popular opinion says—and research supports—that a father shapes the personality, self-esteem, and relationship views of his daughter. In the next chapter, we'll do a didactic review of my father, my view on father-daughter relationships, and how that view has made me who I am today.

Chapter Five

HOW TO RESOLVE FATHERLESS DAUGHTER PAIN

"And my God will supply all your needs
according to His riches in glory in Christ Jesus."
Philippians 4:19 (NASB), Apostle Paul

FATHER-DAUGHTER RELATIONSHIP

A guy said to me once, "Anita, my mother told me not to date you because you didn't have a good relationship with your father."

My response was, "Ok—so is that the decision you've made?" I could tell that wasn't the answer he was expecting. He looked up at me from his plate as if he expected me to launch into an explanation justifying why I never talked about my father. I looked back at him to confirm I felt no explanation or justification was needed. I surely wasn't going to interview for a position for which I had not applied. Either he accepted my friendship without the information or he moved on to spend time with someone else. We quietly finished our dinner.

The role of a father in a daughter's life is in fact a very important one. Research supports the idea that father-daughter relationships shape a daughter's view of men and even influence her decision regarding the type of man she will marry. More recent research supports the idea that the father-daughter relationship significantly affects her self-esteem, self-confidence, body image, academic achievement, and occupational success. Daughters that are fathered by men that are loving, encouraging, and present feel better about themselves, earn higher grades, and experience more success in their careers. Both research studies are discussed further below.

The Journal of Black Psychology published the findings of a study by S.M. Cooper in November 2009 titled "Associations Between Father-Daughter Relationship Quality and the Academic Engagement of African American Adolescent Girls: Self-Esteem as a Mediator?" that showed the positive relationship between girls' academic achievement and the quality of the father-daughter relationship. It went on to state the importance of the quality of the relationship between a father and a daughter to her self-esteem.

In 1990, Dr. Linda Nielsen of Wake Forest University created a college course to focus specifically on father-daughter relationships. The course content was exclusively written to review and explore this one subject. Through the course she conducted a fifteen-year study, collecting data from the girls that took her class. In a post titled "How Dads Affect Their Daughters into Adulthood" shared on *The Blog of the Institute of Family Studies*, Dr. Nielsen stated that through her studies she's learned "daughters whose fathers were actively engaged in their life throughout childhood are more likely to graduate from college and to enter higher paying, more demanding jobs traditionally held by males." They become more tenacious, self-disciplined, and ambitious. They're "less likely to get pregnant as a teenager and less likely to become sexually active in their early teens." Dr. Nielsen goes on to say a "well-fathered daughter is most likely to have relationships with men that are emotionally intimate and fulfilling, in addition to more satisfying, long-lasting marriages." Surprisingly, she found that fathers generally have more impact on daughters than mothers do. So the concern of my friend's mother was well-founded, just not well applied.

No, my relationship with my bio-father was not a good one. He was a nonfunctioning, homicidal alcoholic that could often be found highly inebriated and committing adultery. Though he was residentially in the home, we rarely had a conversation. Many people emotionally argue that I could not have had the intellectual capability to ascertain whether or not my father was a good father when I was five years old, but by the age of five it was obvious, I'd had enough. How could I know at such a young age that he wasn't a good father? This next story should answer that.

TRUE STORY
SOUTHERN SWINGS

Many mornings, after she'd finished her eleven-to-seven night shift at the hospital, my mother, a registered nurse, would pick me up from whichever relative or neighbor's home I'd stayed the night before and we'd go home. The ride home was generally a quiet one, though I'd be wondering what fiasco we'd walk into that day and why my mother wouldn't just leave my father. Every morning there was something. He was either primed on ready-set-go for a fight with her, or he would have made a royal mess in the kitchen—a mess worthy of the skill of a hotel cleaning staff.

Entering through the back door on this particular morning, we found raw eggs and half-cooked grits spilled from one side of the kitchen to the other, so my mama changed out of her uniform and started cleaning. Usually when we came home to a mess like that, I'd just go into the den and turn on the television, a worn routine of subconscious action. Well, this morning, I walked past the TV, through the living room, out the front door and I kept walking. I was five years old. Even at such a young age, I knew this wasn't it. This wasn't living. It sure wasn't an abundant life.

As I walked that morning, with no thought of where to go, I saw airplanes in the sky and daydreamed about how far away I could go in those planes. It's amazing to think back on that day and realize not one neighbor saw me. In the South, that was a miracle. People were either outside being the news or in the window watching somebody else be the news. It was the top of the morning, prime time for retired neighbors to be in their gardens, for mothers to be headed to work, for husbands to be headed home, and for kids to be outside playing, but I ran into no one.

I managed to walk about six blocks unseen and ended up at the neighborhood park. If I'd known the paths to follow through side streets, it wouldn't have been that far, but I was five years old. All I knew were the driving routes—which made the park six blocks away—so that's the way I walked.

Hopping onto one of the swings, I gripped the chain. As I swung back and forth, I giggled as I felt the thrust of air whisk by my ears, my little legs moving back and forth to propel the arc of the swing higher. It's the first time I remember hearing the sound of my own laughter. As I swung higher and higher, I felt like there was nothing I couldn't do. I could see farther and farther and felt innocence, one with a purpose to take on the world. I thought about the airplanes I'd seen and imagined that was what it felt like to be on one. It felt so good. I was free. Until …

I heard someone yelling. At first I couldn't make out what he was saying but he was waving for me to come. "Girl, your mama looking for you." It was a neighbor, yelling across the softball field at me. "Everybody's looking for you. You better come on!" Like air from a balloon, my swing slowed to a pitiful half twist and my giggling stopped. *Why? Do I have to go back there?*

All I wondered for months, which seemed like years to a five-year-old, was when I would be free again. The following weekend, I was taken to my grandparents' house in the country. I asked my grandfather, Big Daddy, when would I be free again? He just smiled. I never did get an answer out of him and that was rare. He was the one person I could always depend on for a straight and honest answer. Big Mama, on the other hand, asked me where was I in such a hurry to go. Sitting over soggy Cheerios I had no intention of eating, I replied, "Somewhere else."

Given that story is one of my major family memories, on the surface it appears I was not well-fathered. But let's look more granularly at the duties and definition of a father.

WHAT IS A FATHER?

We expect fathers to be providers, teachers, encouragers, protectors, and friends, among other things. As we grow up, each role takes on a different meaning. For example, a provider to an infant, who doesn't ask for much, is different from a provider to a teenager, who will ask for the moon. Fathers teach us how to ride bicycles and drive cars. They protect us by putting training wheels on our bicycles, purchasing insurance for the car, and encouraging us to follow our dreams.

Now what is the definition of a father? Defining who and what a father is can be a point of contention. People unpack a lot of emotional baggage when it comes to defining a father, and that baggage makes itself at home in their lives. They willingly and voluntarily store and carry or wheel around bitterness in that emotional baggage, bitterness that was created through the process of holding someone responsible for failing to perform in a position they were never qualified to fill. If I had a nickel for every time I heard a client justify their bad behavior by telling me they didn't have a father, I would have retired at age twenty-seven. If this is you —please stop allowing someone else's shade to block your shine.

Wikipedia has eighteen different definitions describing biological and non-biological fathers, covering everything from current pop-culture vernacular to Quebec civil law. The most interesting of these definitions were DI Dad ("donor insemination"), Presumed Father ("probable but not yet proven"), and Social Father ("assuming de facto responsibility"). We may chuckle, but if many of us would just accept the multitude of social fathers we were blessed to have, it would lift a tractor-trailer sized emotional burden off our shoulders. We had uncles, older cousins, coaches, neighborhood dads, grandfathers, and godfathers. But all their efforts to fill us with wisdom and all the benefits of the lessons they taught us are lost simply because they weren't the genetic contributor.

LESSON TO LEARN

Even though my biological father tried to kill me, and his homicidal attempts helped shaped my withdrawal from family, I did harness valuable lessons from other elders. As I stated in chapter two, you had some bad things happen in your life but the good things you experienced are just as much a part of you. I can say that, fortunately, the elder men in my life that were positive influences were present for the most important years, the formative ones, and no one can take that away from me.

Take an honest look back through your past. Find the positive male role models and be thankful for the social fathers that are responsible for helping you get this far.

THE FIGHT FOR HEALTHY

Enduring difficult situations is sorrowful, but at some point we must decide to move on. We must decide to write a new story for our lives. We must make the conscious choice to seek a joyful future over a painful past and if you are a fatherless daughter, right here is one of the best places to start applying it.

If you have *any* fatherless daughter baggage, I beg you to consider the positive male role models you *did* have. Take your time with this one and dig deep. Leave no one out. Consider teachers, church members, and celebrities—yes, even celebrities. Though you may have never met them personally, it is possible their words of wisdom ("pearls of protection" I like to call them) affected your life in a positive manner. It could have been a speech they gave at a fundraiser you attended or the reason they decided to accept or deny a certain acting role. Dig—and dig deep—I'm sure you'll find at least five.

My "father" is a collage of my two grandfathers and my uncles (my godmother's brothers) with a host of other Catholic Church elders, teachers, college professors, and coaches. I grew up during a time when, if one of us (playmates, classmates, friends, etc.) got into trouble, all of us were in trouble. It was so unlike today: almost everyone was free to give you advice, to discipline you, and to tell you what they thought of you. It was simpler then because everyone had the same goal, the same morals, and the same values when it came to children.

Unlike the healthy women in my life who approved of me or disciplined me with words, the men in my life did it with their eyes and, if I did something real good, a pat on the head. I can think of many times the church elders, teachers, and coaches approved, congratulated, or even warned me so that I wouldn't require discipline. But nothing sticks out like the lesson from my grandfather, Uncle Sam. (My bio-father's parents died when he was young, and he was taken in by relatives; therefore I didn't call him "grandfather," but "uncle"; nevertheless, he did the job.)

He and I were sitting at the kitchen table, waiting for my grandmother to serve us lunch. I was swinging my legs back and forth under the table. I was so small my feet didn't touch the floor yet. He had a small flower tucked behind his ear, smaller than the roses or carnations I was used to seeing him carry. Noticing me noticing the rosebud, he removed it from behind his ear and said to me, "You are just like this rose—small and beautiful, but delicate and only with the right amount of nourishment will you open up and allow your true beauty to show. You stay just like *that*." The impact of that one statement continues to multiply blessings in my life even today. It contains countless compliments and insight into who I am as a person, and it encourages me to maintain my individualism.

With my other grandfather, Big Daddy, it wasn't so much what he said, but what he allowed me to do. While Big Mama said, "Don't leave the yard," Big Daddy let me roam the countryside. At any time on any given day, I could be two or three acres over, which was a couple of houses down in any direction. I wish he was alive today. I'd love to know what he saw in me at such a young age that confirmed for him I was strong and determined.

He and Big Mama lived on a farm with a pecan tree, a fig tree, pigs, hogs, chickens, corn, a slew of vegetables, and acres of land. Big Daddy was a Mason, a leader in the church, and an elder in the community. Many nights, men in the community would stop by for his counsel.

One afternoon, when I was about seven or eight years old, a gentleman stopped by with his horse and asked Big Daddy if his grandkids wanted to ride. Of course, my cousins started jumping up and down in excitement to get a chance to ride the horse, but not me. I sat down in the grassy middle section of the dirt road and watched as each of my cousins was put on the horse and guided to the end of the lane and back, one by one.

When the horse was being led back with the last cousin, Big Daddy looked over at me and asked, "You gone ride?"

I deliberated for a second, then answered, "Nahhhh."

The gentleman asked if he should stop on his way back later in the day to see if I had changed my mind.

Big Daddy chuckled and replied, "No, if *that* one tells you no, it's going to be no when you come back."

Social fathers can play vital roles in your life if you hold onto the lessons they taught you and let go of the pain festering from whatever your bio-father was or was not. Concentrate on the love you received from your social fathers. They have certainly provided many pivotal moments for me to learn and grow from, and the pivotal moments involving my social fathers have elevated me every time. They provided a solid understanding of men, God, and the circle of life.

For example, men show love through action and trust. Big Daddy knew I wasn't a follower. He knew that whatever mischief found me, I was strong and determined enough to walk away, so he trusted me to roam from acre to acre, house to house. He also made homemade, manually churned ice cream every time I asked for it. Hand churned with vanilla extract, fresh picked strawberries or peaches, and cream made from scratch. I have known no greater love.

The most recent—and I'd say biggest—lesson I've learned thus far is to stop underestimating myself. I learned I had to stop lying around, waiting on my expiration date. I had to let my little light shine, whether others accepted my intellect or not. I realized this twenty years after a graduate school professor/social father made a statement to me; it started to resonate again, over and over.

After class one night in graduate school at Virginia State University, I was expressing my displeasure with people to my professor, Dr. Samuel Creighton. I was telling him how much I hate people and I was fit to be tied because I was so sick and tired of people treating me like I was stupid, when Dr. Creighton said, "Anita, people don't treat you like you're stupid—you treat people like they're smart." I was frozen and stricken with silence. Twenty years after that statement was made, I finally fully understood and accepted his statement for truth. What can I say? I'm a slow learner. In 2014, I decided to shed all the "they say" and "supposed to be" and just be me, to let people get to know the real me, whether it goes with the status quo or not.

7-STEP
METHOD AFFIRMATION

I am precious.

7-STEP METHOD TECHNIQUE
CELEBRATING SELF

Surely, along the way, you've had a celebration or two in your life. Remember how that made you feel? What happened? Why did you stop celebrating you? It's as important to our emotional health as food and water are to our physical health. We must consistently celebrate ourselves. It feeds our soul and fuels our feeling of worthiness. It ensures we walk tall versus slumped. With each passing year, the less you celebrate, the less you care for yourself, outwardly and inwardly. A celebration does not require a room full of guests, a 14k-gold charger, and a plated meal. It simply requires love and admiration. It's an appointed time to pat yourself on the back and feel the positive energy of being adored and appreciated—by you.

If you're the woman that says, "I have to take care of my kids first," what will they remember about their mom if she is always blending into the background? You're their first female role model—shine!

7-STEP METHOD ACTIVITY
CELEBRATING SELF

This activity has one requirement—it has to be something you've never done before. It has to be something you will find invigorating. Ok, that's two requirements, but you get my point.   Can't think of anything? I've got suggestions. Go to ThatAnitaLive.com/bk1 and download the free resources. In the pack is a Celebrating Self Tip Sheet. Remember, something you've never done before!

BONUS ACTIVITY
FINDING MY FATHER COLLAGE

Stack a deck of index cards. Taking one card at a time, write the name of a male elder in your life on one side of the card, one name per card. Start with family members, then family members of friends, then coaches, teachers, professors, coworkers, customers, etc. Go through every year of your life and write down every name you can remember. Next, go through the cards one by one, reading the name on the front and writing on the back a lesson the person taught you or a profound statement they said to you. It could be good or bad. Just write it down. Now, go back through the cards, reading only the side of the card with the lesson or profound statement. Stack the good to the left and the bad to the right. Collect the stack on the left and read the side with the names. These men make up your Social Father. You can even collect copies of pictures of them and make a collage, using various parts of their faces.

COMING UP NEXT

Have you seen those people that can stay calm in the midst of chaos? Ever wonder how they learn to do it? In the next chapter we discuss exactly how to become the master of your emotions and learn to never allow anyone to push your buttons again.

Chapter Six

HOW TO MASTER YOUR EMOTIONS

"I am the master of my fate, I am the captain of my soul."
"Invictus" William Ernest Henley

THE BALANCER IS PEACE

If you have anything in life you care about, sooner or later it will spin out of control or come under attack. Learning to center yourself is a skill you will need to keep a cool head. As you put the principles and techniques I've shared in this book to work in your life, remember the key to success is balance. In all things—your challenges, setbacks, gains, successes, transformations, and transitions—always remember to take personal quiet time to be alone with you. This is the time-tested exercise that will keep you balanced. Take time alone to sit and think of nothing, time where you sit and do nothing. It creates space in your life for emotional expansion.

For me, the best time is right after writing in my journal. I've dumped information and concerns from my mind onto paper, so I'm clear to just breathe and be. This exercise will help you remain calm and in control of your emotions and actions when everything else is busting loose.

If you find nothingness hard, concentrate on your breathing. In a quiet space, close your eyes and take long, slow, deep breaths. As your lungs inflate and deflate with air, picture the air going into your throat, down into your lungs, and back out the same path. Picture your chest rising and falling with every breath. A few of my clients listen to instrumental music during their quiet time—slow, methodical, instrumental music. It helps them focus, concentrate, and get centered.

You may already have so much in the air you've forgotten the word *peace* exists. Kids, a demanding supervisor, nosy in-laws, student loans, narcissistic mother, church ministry, exes, social club, unsupportive spouse, exercise, overdue bills, vitamins, crazy neighbors, guilt-dripping grandma, car repairs, nonworking coworkers, stop-n-go traffic, step-kids, late subway trains, home owners' associations, abusive siblings, college tuition, etc. It all gets to be too much at times. That's why it's important to have in your life a very basic thing we all take for granted—peace.

TRUE STORY
TRUE LOVE

Inner peace and quiet can also be obtained from good memories of sincere love. When you recall a good memory of someone who loved you unconditionally, notice the feeling of warmth and joy that fills your body. It's a great feeling that can be used to center yourself when things go awry. The only time I experienced any type of peace in my childhood was when I was with one of my elders. Those to whom this book is dedicated. While I attended school in the town limits, I actually grew up in the country, *grew* being the operative word. Those memories of growing up on Catholic Hill are where I pull calm energy from to this day. There is no better ice cream than fresh made hand-churned ice cream made with farm-grown fruit, and there is no better feeling than watching it be made every time you ask for it without fail. Do you know how hard it is to grind large blocks of ice by hand? That's love and remembering that love is peaceful.

Grew is the operative word because, as a small child, as I skipped back and forth under my Aunt Earline's clothesline as she put out sheets to dry or took them in, there was no dream or goal that I could tell her that was too big or impossible. I would tell her about how I was going to have a housekeeper and a driver, and an airplane would take me back and forth to work, and she never once uttered a sound or word of doubt or discouragement. She lived in that world of future pretense right along with me. She'd ask me what the color of the car would be or if she could get a ride on the plane or if the cook could make her a few meals. She expanded my mind and my soul. That's love and remembering that love is peaceful.

Grew is the operative word because when Big Mama served Cheerios for breakfast, without fail I refused to eat it every time. She tried to make me sit there until I did eat it but when Big Daddy came in from the farm for lunch he'd dismiss me. Nobody wants to look upon the long face of a child while they try to enjoy their meal. Being dismissed, I'd run about a hundred yards to my Aunt Pearline's house, jump the ditch, front yard, and porch in three steps while I yelled her name. She'd meet me at the screen door. Running into her house, I'd ask, "Aunt Pearline, you had breakfast yet?" hitting every syllable and knowing full well breakfast hours in the country were long over. She'd respond to my pouting,

"Marylena ain't feed that baby this morning?"

"No!"

"Come on in the kitchen, let's see what we could find for that baby to eat. Marylena know she supposed to feed my baby!"

In ninety-eight degree heat and eighty percent humidity, she'd boil grits, scramble eggs, and fry bacon till I was full as a tick and couldn't eat another bite. Then we'd watch TV for a few hours and share a Nestle Butterfinger for dessert. Being nurtured and fussed over was endearing to the soul. It taught me I mattered. It taught me I was loved and that love is peaceful.

Grew is the operative word because I didn't need money on The Hill. Snack time meant I simply walked over to my Cousin Henrietta's corner store and asked for what I wanted. The lessons I learned during those years are priceless, even when they were painful. See, one day I moseyed into her store and there was a new stand. At the top of the stand was a shiny new bright yellow top. Inside were what looked to be a million individually wrapped big red balls.

"Cousin Henrietta, what's this?"

"You don't want that."

"But what is it?"

She kept reading her newspaper and didn't answer. My six-year-old curiosity was piqued, and I couldn't look at anything else. I was fascinated. They weren't Now & Laters or Chick-o-Sticks or Mr.

Goodbars, so what were they? I changed my tactic.

"Can I have one?"

"Didn't I tell you you don't want that?" she exclaimed.

I didn't give up. I asked again and again until she relented.

"Yes!" I tiptoed to be able to remove the yellow top and reach my hand into the jar. Cousin Henrietta disappeared into the back of the store. I tore open the wrapper and started to eat the candy. About fifteen seconds later when that Atomic Fireball candy lit my mouth up, I learned a very important and valuable lesson—I was loved. Because through the water that was building up in my eyes, I saw Cousin Henrietta standing before me with an ice cold soda. That is love and love is peaceful. Learn to identify what is and what is not love. The earlier you can identify the difference, the more you can experience a state of calm and contentment.

Many times I reach back into my memory bank of good memories to stop negative thoughts or anxiety in its tracks. It takes practice, but come up with three or four memories of your own that make you remember being loved and that make you feel loved. It will help you master inner peace and quiet.

Perfecting the skill of balancing your inner peace will make you the master of your emotions and prevent anyone from pushing your hot buttons and making you respond uncontrollably. To become the master of your emotions, you must know how to surrender and be vulnerable emotionally. The same is true when it comes to being emotionally healthy: you must be able to approach life with an open heart, a willing spirit, and a healed soul. I'm willing to bet your instinct will not allow you to be vulnerable or surrender. Emotionally, you're constantly blocking and jabbing like a boxer in the ring to protect your feelings, or you're constantly coming up with smart-alecky quick-witted responses in anticipation of future verbal confrontations, or you're loud and boisterous, always on ready-set-go, popping off for a fight with anybody at any time. That is not living in peace. Constantly blocking and jabbing and nurturing negative thoughts drains you of much-needed energy. Energy you need to bring yourself back to center.

LESSON TO LEARN

Had I started my journey to emotional wellness earlier, Legion would have never had a chance to commit the acts he did. I wasn't meditating. I wasn't remembering the good but fighting to forget the bad.

Taking the time to meditate on good memories cleanses the soul of dysfunctional traumas and creates clean space in your emotions for new experiences, for happiness. Cleansing your soul is so important because it affects your ability to mature, prosper, and experience fulfilling relationships. It affects your ability to experience pure joy—the kind of joy that comes from within, from deep within the core of your being. It is the definition of what makes you bloom with expressive beauty. Your eyes dance. Your nose crinkles. Your cheeks glow. Your voice releases the sounds of chuckles and giggles. It's different from person to person. But to fully live life, you must be able to master your emotions, you must be able to control your inner peace and quiet. So the next time negatively flows into your mind, close your eyes, breathe slow, and feel happy. How? By remembering happier times.

7-STEP
METHOD AFFIRMATION

I am peace. I am peaceful. I am at peace.

7-STEP METHOD TECHNIQUE
INNER PEACE AND QUIET

The guide for your future uses the core within you as a compass. It's called your instinct. Some refer to it as intuition. But it is the one thing God uses to tell you when to move and where to go. If you can't feel your instinct, if you are always second-guessing yourself, it is because you have too much clutter in your life. Clutter comes in the form of noise from negative news programs, constantly checking social media, always being busy, experiencing one life-altering error after another. We all have short-term and long-term memories. Once the negativity is received, it is bound to affect your emotions, good or bad. Therefore, limit your negative intake. Your inner peace and quiet rests at your core. Your pulse keeps the beat and your mind keeps the melody of your peace. If you're ever wondering whether you are at peace, check your pulse and your mind. If either of those is moving at a swift pace, like a pinball machine, bells, whistles and all, you're not at peace.

7-STEP METHOD ACTIVITY
INNER PEACE AND QUIET

Exercising deep breathing in a quiet environment is the easiest way to begin to enter a peaceful state. To maintain that peace and become the master of your emotions is not easy but doable. The trick is to catch what is triggering your emotions and maintain control. Never let it get beyond your grasp. Simple right? It does take some practice. On a piece of paper, write down the last five incidents that caused you to lose your composure and become uncontrollably angry. Once a week, sit down alone with this list and recall them one by one. Identify the "trigger"—what was the belief that made you lose control? The more you practice, the quicker you will be able to catch the trigger and maintain a peaceful state, so that when the same trigger happens in a different situation, you can catch it and keep your cool.

Chapter Seven

HOW TO MAKE PROGRESS

"Sometimes making progress a step at a time
is better than no progress at all."
"Taking His Own Path, He Follows His Father,"
New York Times, July 17, 1998, Evan Bayh

OPTIONS

You will repeat what you opt not to resolve. Plain and simple, you will have to fight to be healthy. It will be a struggle. You will struggle with your internal self because you've been conditioned to respect titles. This level of respect has taught us to hold on to the connotation of a word, even if it means accepting being treated poorly by the person in the position. For example, let's say your mother constantly belittles you, blames you for the failures of your siblings, and never keeps her word. Or your sister calls you names, intimidates and threatens you. Because these two people have the titles "mother" and "sister," society has trained us to smile like everything is ok and pretend all is well. You will struggle with guilt because the abuser will attempt to continue the negative cycle. You will struggle with others that feel their ten minutes of exposure to your dysfunctional family trumps your years of personal experience, and they will give you unsolicited advice. You will struggle because you want everything to appear perfect to friends and neighbors. You will struggle because people will feel threatened by your growth and attempt to force you to stay in their comfort zone. *You must choose.*

As you work toward creating your new emotionally healthy life, challenges and obstacles will come. You have to guard your own emotional security. At times, it will feel like everything is working against you and holding you back from peace and from all the greatness within you that you are destined to share with the world. At times you will be able to feel the push and pull of the contradiction happening within you. You may even experience a setback. But as the ole saying goes, when we know better we do better, so when you realize you have fallen back into your old ways, get up and do better.

Consider what it would be like to be surrounded by people that are all for you! People that encourage you and want to see you grow, want to see you win, want to see you get the best out of life and all it has to offer. People that aren't jealous of you or intimidated by you. People that aren't trying to take advantage of you. People that are "down" for you and "have your back," come what may! Choosing to surround yourself with loyal people means you're choosing self-care, which means you're choosing what's important. It means you're choosing you. You've cleared space in your life for healing by disposing of distractions, and you've cleared space in your life for emotional maturity. Don't lose it. Fight to stay healthy.

At one point in 2017, my mother and brother contacting my coworkers, colleagues, and service professionals became so distressing, I had to send them written No Contact Orders. I became so enraged I almost returned to my childhood home to solve this problem the way they handle all issues, by shouting and fighting. But I didn't. I fought for healthy. I chose to sit in peace and quiet and remember being loved. Though I felt like prey being circled by buzzards itching at the opportunity to pounce and devour, I chose to stay on the path of emotional maturity and not lose the gains I'd made thus far. I just accepted that people that never thought anything of me will never think anything of me, no matter how great I become.

You have to keep a level head to prevent them from getting the best of you and causing catastrophic setbacks. You have to do what is best for you in the time and space you can control. And you can do this. You have the ability to accomplish your wildest dreams and then some! Everything you have persevered through to get this far has prepared you for what is to come. Remember the last time you made up your mind that you were going to win—and you did? This is no different. It may be a bigger dream and it may take a little longer to obtain, but in the end, if you don't give up, it will all be yours.

LESSON TO LEARN

My grandfather use to say that when a chicken gives an egg it's a donation, when a pig gives ham, it's a sacrifice. To what are you giving your future—a donation or a sacrifice? For the changes you want to see happen in your life, you must be intentional. You must have a plan, and you must take action. Nothing changes unless you move with the intention to make the change. Yes, it requires sacrifice. As you grow, you will leave behind old behaviors, old activities; you will no longer find enjoyment in them. As you mature, you will leave behind people that are not growing with you. Oh, they'll squawk about you being different. They may even make fun of you, but I encourage you to keep going! Life is about growth and change and when you're no longer maturing, you're just existing. Carrying emotional baggage is like carrying other people's fingerprint smudge on your life. Is that anyway to live? I assure you and I speak from experience, there is more, there is better, and it is available to all of us.

7-STEP
METHOD AFFIRMATION

I am in a perfecting process.

7-STEP METHOD TECHNIQUE
EMOTIONAL EQUATION

Every area of your life is moving as you move—your emotions, your body, your morals, your mind, and your money. Therefore, for you to spiral up in life, all of you must move in tandem motion together. You must live in alignment with your beliefs. You must mature in your decision-making. If not, some part of you will always be pulling the rest of you back. You've seen people that were given an opportunity before they were prepared to handle it. In the biggest opportunity of their life, they awkwardly appear mismatched for the setting by saying the wrong thing or behaving inappropriately. Consider the behavior of some Olympic athletes or the uncle that continues to talk about the one that got away. The level of maturity didn't match the opportunity given. The errors can be life altering. Don't make that mistake. The Emotional Equation is designed to help you put forth the effort to mature in every area of your life annually.

7-STEP METHOD ACTIVITY
EMOTIONAL EQUATION

Being the geek that I am, I have designed an Emotional Equation to help you mature. You can review your life by solving for the answers to the equation as often as you like: monthly, quarterly, or annually. It is totally up to you. The Emotional Equation is a way to assess whether or not your decision-making is in accordance with your morals and values. See, most of the time, our morals and values (you know, those things we use to judge others) are much more mature than the daily decisions we make. Are you measuring yourself by the same measure with which you critique others? If we checked your social media posts, I bet the answer would be no.

The equation:

$\frac{EMPF}{S}$ = CONTINUOUS EMOTIONAL MATURITY

On a very high level, to solve the Emotional Equation, first, you are going to set goals in four areas: Emotional Management, Mental Clarity, Physical Fitness, and Fiscal Fitness. Then you will begin the work it takes to accomplish those goals by making decisions that are in line with your spiritual beliefs, your morals, and your values. Every major religious denomination has these four areas as important practices of living a good life. You can set monthly, quarterly, or annual goals, that is up to you, but you must do something toward obtaining them every day.

EMOTIONAL MANAGEMENT

Emotional Management is your ability to control the emotion you're feeling by checking your emotional reaction against reality and choosing an appropriate response. For example, a wife, let's call her Jill, leaves home with plenty of driving time to pick up her husband, Jack, from work. On her way, she's caught in a traffic jam and has to follow a detour due to an accident. She is unfamiliar with the detour route. Her stress level goes through the roof. When she finally reaches Jack's job, he hops in the car, kisses her on the cheek, and asks why she's late. Jill burst into tears and screams about how mean Jack is being to her. Is this an accurate response? Of course not. Jill's response is a reaction to the fear of getting lost and being harmed, not Jack's question. She could learn to better manage her emotions. How? The short answer is by becoming more self-aware. The long answer is by setting a measureable goal of being able to control her response to fear within six months, choosing a technique to help her improve her ability to react to the fear she is being challenged with, practicing the technique, and then evaluating her growth in her quiet time. Replays is a technique that can be used to strengthen your ability to control your reactions. Here's how, in four easy steps: (1) Schedule quiet time alone every day to reflect on your latest event and replay it in your mind as if you are watching it unfold. (2) Take note of the moments your emotions change by writing down the emotion you're feeling and, in three words or less, the cause of the change in emotions. Not when you remember them changing, but when you feel them change. (3) Identify what you are afraid of. (4) Practice the following statement, inserting your words appropriately: "I felt (insert emotion) when (cause of change) happened because I feared (insert what you feared)." In Jill's case, her statement may go something like this, "I felt anxious when the traffic had to detour because I feared getting lost and being harmed." This practice will help you communicate your emotions, instead of acting them out. You'll be the master of your emotions in no time.

MENTAL CLARITY

Having a cluttered mind is the same as trying to work in a cluttered space. Have you ever tried to walk down a narrow hallway that has boxes of different sizes piled up on both sides? Flaps hanging, paper dropping out onto the floor, some boxes turned horizontal and others turned vertical. Not easy to maneuver, is it? Having a clear mind is like having a clean empty room in which to work. It allows your creative juices to flow freely.

For some abuse survivors, the cluttered space in their mind is the tape of past abuse that plays at the most inopportune moment. It plays things like, who do you think you are, you ain't nothing now and you ain't gon' be nothing, you're ugly, you're fat, you're too dark skinned, you're too skinny, your eyes are too small, you're stupid, you could never do that.

Remarkably enough, the tape usually plays in the voice of the person that made those impactful statements. No matter who it was that said it, mental clarity is paramount to living an emotionally healthy life. My all-time favorite technique for clearing the mind is journaling. You could set a goal of clearing your mind once every day and enjoying an activity in the moment without thinking about or worrying about anything else. Write in your journal everything that comes to mind. Don't edit, just write. Continue to write until nothing comes to mind. Then go for a walk, enjoying the view along the way, or spend time with a loved one but remain in the moment. For some, writing in their journal once in the evening before bed time is enough. For me, I'd carry my journal with me all day writing whenever I couldn't focus. Do what works best for you.

PHYSICAL FITNESS

A friend of mine would always refer to the systems of the body as if they were the systems of a house. The nerves were the electrical system. The intestines were the plumbing system. The bones were the framing and the muscles were the walls. In a house, these systems are interdependent; the same is true for the body. If one is damaged or nonfunctioning, it affects the health of the others. To live an emotionally healthy life, you must also care for the body that houses the emotions, and physical fitness is a treasure trove of goals. There is so much to choose from: weight loss, muscle toning, blood pressure, hydration, endurance, metabolism, vitamin intake, sodium intake management, sugar intake management, and on and on. A good place to start before deciding on your goal is your doctor. During your yearly physical, ask for suggestions on where you can improve your health. Make one of those suggestions your goal. You could even join a gym or hire a physical trainer or nutritionist to help you. Those people eat, sleep, and breathe goals.

FISCAL FITNESS

We all love having a positive cash flow, but it doesn't happen magically. It takes discipline to manage the inward and outward flow of cash. Sometimes you have to tell yourself no, and denying ourselves from impulsive decisions hurts. But maintaining a balance between your wants and needs is possible and you can do it. You just need to learn how to apply delayed gratification, sacrificing what you want now for what you need later. Really, between you and me, it comes down to asking yourself, how bad do you want it and what are you willing to do to get it?

Here are a few things you can do to monitor your cash flow and keep it positive. 1) Track your income, 2) Track your spending, 3) Set measurable fiscal goals, 4) Be able to tell a want from a need, 5) Plan ahead, 6) Learn from your mistakes, and 7) Refocus quarterly. It sounds like a lot, but it's not because the actions to carry them out overlap. If you need some how-to information, here it is...

First, to track your income and your spending, write down every penny. The easiest way I've found to do it is per action in a Transaction Log or Check Register. Each time you receive money or spend money, you write it down. At the end of thirty days, type all of your income and expenditures into a spreadsheet. Label five columns across the top – Date, Item, Category, Kind, and Amount. As you enter the entries from your register into the spreadsheet, first place the date you received or spent the money. If it was income, label it income, but if it was an expenditure, label it according to what it was spent on: snacks, water bill, violin lessons, etc. In the third column, type the applicable category from the following list: Housing, Transportation, Personal Debt, Food, Utilities, Clothing (clean/mend), Savings, Insurance, Personal Care, Health, or Relaxation/Entertainment. In the fourth column you're going to identify the item as a want or a need. In the fifth and final column you will enter the dollar amount. After completing this spreadsheet, go back over it and compare columns two and four. Are any of the items you labeled *needs* in column four not labeled as a *bill* in column two? Ask yourself how many of the items can you do without? Stay focused, we're not finished yet.

Now, you're going to calculate a percentage for each Category. This will show you exactly where your money is going and how you can change your spending habits. It will identify where you can set realistic, manageable, measureable fiscal goals. Could you cut back on "want" spending? Could you turn off your cable and funnel those dollars into your savings? What about retirement? Are you saving enough? Those decisions are your decisions, but I'm here if you need any help. Feel free to email or private message me on any social media platform with questions. I'd love to help.

Before we end our discussion on the Emotional Equation, here are a few questions to get you started solving for your own personal answers to the equation:

First, what is the moral code by which you live your life? It's your belief of what is right and wrong.

E – Emotional Management – Does your moral code teach you to allow others to control your emotions? How often do you respond appropriately versus overreact?

M – Mental Clarity – Do your spiritual beliefs teach that you are to mentally live in confusion and clutter? Are you able to clear your mind and maintain a peaceful state of being?

P – Physical Fitness – Do your spiritual beliefs state you should be careless with your physical health? Are you physically healthy?

F – Fiscal Fitness – Do your spiritual beliefs dictate that having debt is good? Do you have a positive net worth?

Chapter Eight

HOW TO SUSTAIN PROGRESS

"Gratitude is the single most important ingredient
to living a successful and fulfilled life."
-Jack Canfield (@JackCanfield, July 13, 2013)

FEELING GRATITUDE

It is not my intent to lead you around by the nose and tell you what to do. However, it is my intent to inform and educate you. It is my intent to show you chapters of my history so that you can recognize the similarity to your own, and then share techniques you can use to repair your hurt and broken places. This is important because if you don't know your history, if you aren't present of mind about your past, you're bound to repeat it.

If your family experiences have been similar to mine, there is one more point I need you to understand before I go. Gratitude facilitates healing, it regenerates healthy emotions. Get the picture, though. I'm not referring to a surface-level halfhearted thank-you, the kind we give when someone holds the door for us or compliments our clothing. I'm referring to the feeling of gratitude that makes tears fall from your eyes and your heart full with unspeakable gratefulness. I'm talking about a way of life where you focus on what is good and positive. It's the best way to sustain growth.

Let's look at three reasons practicing gratitude helps you sustain progress. First, it has been scientifically proven that people who are aware of and meditate on the positive things in their life are happier people. Second, being buried in bitterness and negativity blocks your creative flow, but being upbeat and optimistic cause your creativity to expand. It improves your ability to solve problems and overcome difficulties. Lastly, what you meditate on multiplies. If you constantly point out and think about all the things that go wrong in a day, it narrows your view. When you walk around only paying attention to the negative, you are training your mind to only see the negative; therefore, the negative things are all you will see in the future. As you walk through life, stop allowing your first question to be what's wrong here and start asking yourself what's good here. Trust me, I understand it. It's a slippery slope. When I went "No Contact" with my bio-fam, they came out in full force. My brother and my mother started calling and texting any and everybody they could get a phone number or email address for, from people I had gone to kindergarten with to business mentors to service providers to coworkers. It was so demeaning and humiliating. They created such a web of lies and deceit it caused my health to decline. People would gossip and snicker behind my back at work, at church, almost everywhere I went. The tape of insults and belittlement started to play in my head, in their voices. I had to consciously make the effort to repeat Bible verses and memories of good times in my life aloud to myself daily. I would record and play positive uplifting affirmations to listen to while I was driving. I had to fight to sustain the healthy progress I had made. I was tempted to lose control, fight my brother, and yell and scream at my mother, but I didn't. I had decided that by any means necessary I would maintain my growth and sustain my progress.

Practicing gratitude on a daily basis can have a domino effect on your life because positivity yields happiness and happiness yields creativity and creativity produces art, solves problems, and prevents disease. You will cease to live on ready-set-go, always in defense mode. You'll relax and enjoy life at a new level of peace because you're open to continuous growth and progress. We don't anchor down in positions of defense in environments where we feel safe and are having fun. Think about it, when we anchor down in positions of defense, we're constantly coming up with scenarios to protect ourselves. Our bodies shrink and recoil. It's a lot of energy needlessly burned. It distracts us from focusing on how to continue moving forward in life. But when we spend time coming up with fun and creative thoughts, we flourish. Think about the last time you were in a situation where people were jealous of you. Did your mind and spirit feel light and free to create? Did you walk upbeat with your head held high or drag slowly? Did you feel heavy burdened or lighthearted? Did you feel suspicious and fearful or clear and content? Concentrating on the good will keep you aware of all the wonderful things in life you have to be grateful for and, in response, life will give you more for which to be grateful. You'll take better care of you and the things around you. If you really want a better life, if you really want to move forward with your emotional healing, practice gratitude. Think of something you are immensely grateful for, close your eyes, and say thank-you until you feel it in your heart.

Once you know the feeling of gratitude, it is time to give back! It is time for you to pay it forward. Every community has homeless shelters, foster homes, juvenile detention centers, and broken families experiencing high levels of dysfunction. Volunteer! With volunteering we can change our communities by demonstrating and modeling gratitude. As a volunteer, you're not there to teach or enforce but to be the example. You're there just to be, so others can see what it looks like.

LESSON TO LEARN

Hopefully by now you've gotten it. Childhood trauma turns into what? Yes, adult dysfunctional behavior. But what you have now is something good to compare all the abuse to. Because as abuse survivors and emotional baggage carriers, how do we fight the contradiction that happens within? When the negative talk tries to control your behavior, what can you do? You can count your blessings. You can take stock of what you are thankful for. It doesn't matter what it is, how small it is or whether others may consider it to be insignificant—what counts is it matter to you.

7-STEP
METHOD AFFIRMATION

I am receiving goodness and giving greatness back.

7-STEP METHOD TECHNIQUE
LETTERS OF GRATITUDE

Gratitude can be expressed in many forms and there are just as many benefits for the giver as there are for the receiver. The Letters of Gratitude technique generally takes the writer on a roller-coaster ride for two reasons. First, people tend to hold on to and rehash the negative experiences a lot more than the positive, so it takes a deeper dive into the soul to pull up something worth expressing gratitude for. Second, there is a very strong emotional connection between the heart and the head, so as the giver writes their gratitude letter, the heart is cleansed. That is my wish for you, that your heart be cleansed. That you become free to live true to who you are spiritually, emotionally, and mentally. That you heal your soul from the emotional scars you fight through to simply exist every day. And this activity will push you to take steps in the direction of getting that healing.

7-STEP METHOD ACTIVITY
LETTERS OF GRATITUDE

You are going to think back through your entire life and identify three pivotal moments. Three moments where something someone said to you or something someone did for you significantly altered the course of your life for the better. Once you identify the three moments and the three people, you will write a letter to each person(s) reminding them of what they did, telling them how it has affected your life positively, and expressing your deepest, most honest heartfelt thank-you. Yes, you are to mail these letters to their recipients. If you don't have an address, search for them on Google, Facebook, or Twitter. Search for their children or grand-children, then ask for the address you need.

Here is a personal example. I failed Algebra I in my freshman year of high school. There were two black kids in the class and the teacher sat us at the end of the last row in the back of the class and ignored us. She never even called my name for the roll. My sophomore year of high school, the computer assigned me to the exact same teacher for Algebra I again, but my guidance counselor pulled me out of that class the first week of school and assigned me to a teacher that gave a damn. After being reassigned to a different Algebra I class, not only did I sail through high school math, I went on to earn a Bachelor of Science degree in Mathematics. Can you imagine what type of life I would have fallen into if I had not been able to graduate high school? That one move significantly changed the trajectory of my life. To that guidance counselor, I am immensely grateful.

Your turn! Who will you write and why?

Chapter Nine

CONCLUSION

"Whether you think you can or whether
you think you can't, you're right."
-Henry Ford

I HOPE, WISH, AND PRAY

Family dysfunction is physically and emotionally damaging to not only those directly involved but also those indirectly involved. Everyone that sees and hears the abuse is affected. Within our neighborhoods and homes, we must be honest with ourselves and call abuse, abuse. Ignoring or accommodating the behavior condones it. And condoning it encourages it to continue. This is why generational dysfunction plagues our families for centuries.

We see it in the case where the grandfather, father, and son are all alcoholics; where the grandmother, mother, and daughter have low self-esteem and use manipulation and intimidation to relate to and interact with others. The people in these positions are not just hurting each other. Fathers have brothers, nephews, nieces, and daughters that are all affected by their behavior. Brothers have sisters and cousins. Moms have sons and walls have ears. You get the picture. It's systemic and reaches far beyond the immediate situation. But there is hope for healing. It requires bold honesty. It requires YOU! We have to begin to address all of the abuse under one roof. Until we do, our communities will continue to suffer.

My hope is that after reading this book you have a clear understanding of the connection between childhood trauma and adult dysfunctional behavior and know that sibling abuse is real and not just harmless rivalry. My wish for those who are carrying the long-lasting effects of abuse is that you take the courageous steps to overcome the control it has on your happiness and create a space to live a life of your own kind of peace and joy. My prayer is that from this moment on, you exercise gratitude and give back, doing your part to make the world a better place.

BEFORE YOU GO

I'd love to hear from you. If you enjoyed this book or received value from it in any way, I'd like to ask you for a favor: would you be kind enough to leave a review for this book? I look forward to connecting with you!

BIBLIOGRAPHY

Caffaro, J.V. & Conn-Caffaro, A. (2005). Treating sibling abuse families. *Aggression and Violent Behavior, 10(5): 604-623.*

Cooper, S.M. (2009). Associations between father-daughter relationship quality and the academic engagement of African American adolescent girls: Self-esteem as a mediator? *Journal of Black Psychology,* 35(4) 495-516.

Kiselica, M.S. & Morrill-Richards, M. (2007). Sibling maltreatment: The forgotten abuse. *Journal of Counseling & Development,* 85(2): 148–160.

Meyers, A. (2015). Lifting the veil: The lived experience of sibling abuse. *Qualitative Social Work,* 16 (3): 333-350.

Nielson, L. (2007). College daughters' relationships with their fathers: A 15 year study.
College Student Journal, 41(1): 112-121.

Nielson, Linda. "How Dads Affect Their Daughters into Adulthood." FamilyStudies.org, The Blog of the Institute of Family Studies, June 3, 2014, https://ifstudies.org/blog/how-dads-affect-their-daughters-into-adulthood

Skinner, J. and Kowalski, R.M. (2013). Profiles of sibling bullying. *Journal of Interpersonal Violence:* 28(8):1726-1736.

RESOURCES

UNITED STATES

Rape Abuse & Incest National Network (RAINN) Crisis Hotline 1-800-656-HOPE (4673)

National Domestic Violence Hotline 1-800-799-SAFE (7233)

National Suicide Prevention/Crisis Hotline 1-800-273-8255

DOD Safe Helpline 877-995-5247. The phone number is the same in the U.S. and worldwide via DSN.

CANADA

Crisis Services Canada Hotline 1-833-456-4566

7-STEP METHOD
Masterclass

INTERESTED?

JOIN THE LAUNCH NOTIFICATION LIST AT
ThatAnitaLive.com/CoachMe

The ebook loved by countless readers now has a companion masterclass and community. You don't have to go it alone. Facing your past can be scary, but in the 7-Step Method Masterclass and Community, you'll experience meaningful connections with like-minded women making transformational changes.

Anita Washington, M.Ed. & M.B.A., CEO of That Anita Live, is an abuse survivor herself. Anita knows first-hand how limiting beliefs, self-sabotage and negative thoughts can rob you of enjoying life. In this masterclass she walks you through a step-by-step sequential process to break through years of emotional struggle.

Moreover, the content is broken down into simple easy to understand formats that put you into action immediately. No turning back!

In the 7-Step Method Masterclass you will:

- ✔ Learn to **IDENTIFY** which stage of the Four Life Stages of Emotional Baggage you're in and how to go from stuck to unstoppable

- ✔ Learn how to **DEFY** doubt and build confidence to live authentically in your own personality, spirit and character

- ✔ Learn how to **CREATE** your emotional goals and build a plan to accomplish them

- ✔ Learn how to **RESOLVE** emotional baggage with practical training from people with real life experience.

- ✔ Learn how to **MOVE** immediately into action and have access to one-on-one help with the activities

- ✔ Be **EMPOWERED** and supported by a community of encouragers

- ✔ Learn how to follow a proven success path to find your voice and **DEFINE** your own kind of freedom

LAUNCHING SEPTEMBER 2018

INVITE ANITA WASHINGTON
TO SPEAK OR FACILITATE A WORKSHOP:

Invite me as an expert to speak or facilitate a workshop at your next event. Email anita@thatanitalive.com or direct message me on Facebook/ThatAnitaLive or Twitter.com/ThatAnitaLive, and I'll get back to as soon as possible.

ABOUT THE AUTHOR

ANITA WASHINGTON, M.Ed. & M.B.A., CEO & Founder of That Anita Live, LLC, host of the TV show *That Anita Live* and *The Emotional Happiness Podcast with That Anita Live* provides a platform for women to learn, laugh, and, more importantly, heal.

A former school and community agency counselor and creator of the 7-Step Method, Anita has helped guide people from the ages of eleven to fifty through their own life issues, personal transformations, and professional endeavors. With an old soul and a comedic, honest voice, she uses many southern colloquialisms and colorful expressions to unwrap personal stories of surviving a homicidal alcoholic father, a mother in denial, and four physically and emotionally abusive brothers and relates them to guiding principles and healing techniques.

Through her powerful and uplifting interviews at ThatAnitaLive.TV and *The Emotional Happiness Podcast*, women get to see and hear real women with resourceful stories living relentless lives after life's most devastating events. Through her charismatic and compelling speaking, Anita helps women use the tools and resources they already have to reveal and release success blockers such as childhood trauma and family dysfunction so they can build self-confidence, boost their self-esteem, and feel free to live true to their own personality, spirit, and character.

In her previously released ebook, *7 Simple Steps to Beat Emotional Baggage*, Anita shares actionable techniques that will walk women through letting go of the past and rising above the glass ceiling to reach higher levels of success and satisfaction in life.

Anita is a graduate of Limestone College, Virginia State University, and Strayer University with a B.S. in Mathematics, an M.Ed. in Guidance & Counseling, and an M.B.A. in Contracts & Acquisitions. You can find Anita online at ThatAnitaLive.com, Twitter, Youtube, Instagram, and Facebook. Her handle is That Anita Live on all four social media platforms.

40632211R00121

Made in the USA
Middletown, DE
30 March 2019